徽州老房子
OLD HOUSES OF HUIZHOU

汪森强　著
Wang Senqiang

卢庭芳　摄影
Photography by Lu Tingfang

李长生等　译
Translated by Li Changsheng et al.

Jiangsu Phoenix Fine Arts Publishing House

江苏凤凰美术出版社

东眺宏村　Overlooking Hongcun to the east

目 录
CONTENTS

古朴舒心的家园　Dainty and comfortable home

绿阴翠盖拢南湖　South Lake in shady green

宏村鸟瞰图

Bird's-eye view of Hongcun

承志堂梁枋大型木雕组画

Woodcut drawings on the beams and columns of the Chengzhitang House

家与老房子

　　新买的衣服穿过一段时间，才成了自己的衣服；新置的房子住过一段日子，才成了自己的家。这里，不是产权意义上的权属问题，而是从感情上对新买的东西的认同。

　　一家人在新房子里住下来，房子就成了这户人家的家。年代久了，房子变成了老房子。徽州乡村的老房子，代代相传的多，子孙卖房的少，老房子经历了各个时代的变迁，不但保存了当年的建筑风格，还保存着丰富的历史人文信息，它是家庭和家族的根，也是家园的历史记忆，很宝贵的。

　　徽州，有着二千多年的历史，是中国皖南山区的一处古老的州府，1949年以前管辖着歙县、休宁、黟县、绩溪、祁门、婺源六个县。举世闻名的黄山就坐落在徽州，徽州距离杭州仅有200公里。徽州山多田少，生产的粮食不够当地人食用，徽州各个乡村的男人从小就外出经商，十五世纪中叶到二十世纪中叶的五百年间，徽州的商人遍布全国，取得了巨大的商业成功，成了全国商界的一股强盛的商业势力——徽商。

　　徽商赚了大量的银两，回到家乡大兴土木建新房。徽商不但商业头脑很灵活，而且，社会眼光也很敏锐，城市建筑的新潮流，居住环境的新理念，都很容易被徽商们接受，他们会把城市建筑的新元素带回家乡，把房子造得越来越

老房子里过日子（宏村月沼）　Life in the old house (Crescent Pool, Hongcun)

徽州人家
Household in Huizhou

适宜人居住，一代一代的家也变得越来越舒适。今天，千百个徽州古村落保存下来的成千上万幢老房子，就是当年徽商将银子与城市文明一块带回家乡的文化遗产，是时代文明与传统文化相融合的历史建筑作品，带有强烈的徽州地方特色。徽州古村落的典型代表——黟县的宏村、西递村保存着完整的古村风貌，保存着成片的老房子，它们于2000年11月30日成功登录了世界文化遗产名录，得到了全世界的认可。

作者在宏村的祖屋"树人堂"里生活了六十一年，深深地热爱自己的家乡，也爱村里的老房子，还有探究老房子的浓厚兴趣，经过几年的努力，编写了一本小书：《徽州老房子》，又译成了英文本。希望更多的中外朋友读了书，能多了解徽州的古村建筑，更喜欢中国徽州。

全书分为三章，第一章分析徽州古村的环境、格局和老房子的结构，第二章分析老房子的室内装饰风格，着重介绍典型民居里的木雕图案，第三章着重介绍徽州古村的公共建筑和它的人文价值。书里汇集了大量的古村建筑和自然风光图片，分类归纳分析，突出人与家庭在建筑中留下的人文痕迹，寻觅祖先造房子时营造舒适的家的智慧细节，寻觅当年时代的文明如何融合进当地传统建筑文化里面，提高了家庭生活的质量。不仅仅让读者朋友了解清楚真实的完整的精美的老房子，还要在古村里、在老房子里看到很多当年徽州家庭生活的痕迹，各个时代的社会经济活动的痕迹。既看到老房子，又看到远去的家园，这才是作者写作本书的真正目的和理念。由于作者的才学水平有限，书中会留下不足和遗憾，敬请读者朋友指正。

二〇〇八年一月十八日于宏村树人堂

Home and old houses

Only after one has worn his new clothes for some while can he be said to own the clothes; only after one has lived in a new house for some days can he be said to have his home. This is not an issue of property rights, but an issue of emotional recognition of new purchases.

When a family settles in a new house, the house becomes the home of the family. Many years later, the house becomes an old one. That is the case with the old houses of Huizhou. Most old houses in the villages there have been passed down from ancestral hands without being sold. Even after their vicissitudes over the generations, the houses retain not only the architectural style of the former days, but also rich historical and cultural messages. They are precious: they are the root of family and clan, and historical memories of the home.

Huizhou, with a history of more than 2 000 years, used to be a prefecture in southern Anhui, with six counties, Xixian, Xiuning, Yixian, Jixi, Qimen and Wuyuan, under its administration. The world-renowned Huangshan Mountains is located in Huizhou, an area merely 200 kilometers away from the city of Hangzhou. As Huizhou is mountainous with little farming land, men from the villages of Huizhou do business beyond their villages even when they are in their teens. During the 500 years between the mid-15th and mid-20th centuries, Huizhou merchants were enormously successful across the land: they grew to be a strong

承志堂外院
Courtyard to the Chengzhitang House

commercial force in the business community, and "Huizhou merchants" became a household word.

Many Huizhou merchants returned home with taels in great quantities, and began to build new houses. These merchants not simply had a head for business, but also an eye for societal changes. They readily accepted the new trends of urban architecture and the new ideas of a good living environment. They brought home these new elements from the city and built their houses such that these structures would be more pleasant for human habitation and that the homes would be increasingly comfortable for generation after generation. Today, the millions of old houses preserved from the thousands of old villages of Huizhou constitute the cultural legacy that the merchants of former times brought home with their taels and urban culture. They are works of historical architecture that merges new-age culture with traditional culture, eventually embedded with strong local characteristics of Huizhou. Hongcun and Xidicun, of Yixian County, representatives of these old villages, keep intact their former features, in great stretches. On November 30, 2000, these houses entered *Directory of World Cultural Heritage*, thus receiving worldwide recognition.

The author of this work has lived for 61 years at the Shurentang House, ancestral house of Hongcun. He loves his hometown, and the old houses in the village. With an earnest interest for exploring the old houses, the author spent years and composed this small book, viz., *Old Houses of Huizhou*, complete with an English version. It is hoped that readers from at home and overseas will be better able to understand the old-village architecture of Huizhou and show better love for the place.

The book has three chapters. Chapter One discusses the environment, layout of old villages of Huizhou, and the structure of old houses. Chapter Two addresses the styles of interior decorations of the old houses, with a focus on woodcut patterns in the old houses. Chapter Three covers the public architecture of old villages and their cultural values. This work collects a great number of pictures of old-village architecture and natural sights. These pictures are classified and analyzed, to unveil the cultural traces left behind by man and family, to reveal the details of wisdom with which the ancestral houses were built into comfortable homes, and to explore how the culture of former times fused into the traditional local architecture and improved the quality of family life. The album will not only enable the audience of this book to see the true, intact and elaborate old houses, but to witness the traces of former family life in the old houses, and the traces of socioeconomic activities of the past ages. Seeing the old houses and seeing the distant homes constitutes the very and true purpose and ideology of the author in composing this work. Of course, due to his limited ability, the author must have left behind regrets in the book.

Wang Senqiang
Shurentang House, Hongcun
January 18, 2008

世界文化遗产——宏村、西递村简介

宏　村

宏村位于黟县西北角。南宋绍兴元年（1131），祈墅村汪姓故居焚于兵乱，汪氏六十六世祖汪彦济率全家迁居于雷岗之阳，劈荆斩棘，历经二十年建成十三间楼，定名弘村。清乾隆二年（1737）避帝讳改名宏村。明永乐年间（1403—1424），汪氏七十六世祖汪思齐、胡重夫妇率族人挖水圳，引来西溪水，掘月沼，建总祠，族人陆续下山建房。明万历三十五年（1607），由汪氏八十一世祖汪奎光等十七人主事，历时三年，于村南掘成20247平方米的南湖，清乾嘉年间烟火鼎盛，成了古黟"森然一大都会"。村似牛形。

宏村最出彩的景观是古水系和名宅"承志堂"。水圳引来清泉润万家，防火、浣汲、灌溉家家受益；村心月沼，老屋环峙，半镜中涵，古意盎然，堪称宏村的精品景观；南湖横跨东西，环堤古树，北倚古宅，小径画桥，大片风荷，诗情画意，令人留连。村西豪宅"承志堂"建筑面积3000余平方米，厅堂宽敞，偏厅众多，尤其是前后大厅的雀替、梁枋、门窗上的大幅木雕，幅幅精美，人物栩栩如生，保存完整，素有民间故宫之美誉。

宏村北倚千树雷岗，南临潋滟南湖，村口古树红杨白果，村中月沼水圳，清水长流，老屋鳞次栉比。宏村确是一处水灵景秀、风光宜人的好地方。2000

年11月，宏村登录联合国《世界遗产名录》。

宏村的历史上人才辈出，清朝的文人汪士通、汪文学父子，汪承恩、汪彤雯父子，汪方钟，汪以文，才女汪玢、钱妍等，多有诗文著作传世。官居清朝奉直大夫的汪肇衍、汪兆璋兄弟，曾任民国代理国务总理、国务总理兼财政总长的汪大燮等在官场有善政者，也为家乡增光。著名富商，明代的汪升平，清代的汪授甲、汪家驹兄弟，清末的汪定贵等都为村庄的公共建设慷慨捐资，为世人留下了南湖书院、三立堂、承志堂等幢幢豪宅。

西递村的胡文光牌坊，建于1578年，明朝神宗皇帝表彰功臣胡文光而建。
Hu Wenguang Archway, built in 1578 in honor of Hu Wenguang, minister of Emperor Shenzong of the Ming.

西递村

西递村，古名西川，地处古徽州府之西，曾设驿站"铺递所"而得名，距黟县县城8公里。西递始祖为唐昭宗李晔之子，因遭变乱，被婺源考川人胡三带回家乡养育，改姓胡，名昌翼。昌翼22岁中明经科举，后世称昌翼公"唐太子明经胡始祖"。明经胡五世祖胡士良于北宋元丰年间(1078—1085)定居西递程家里降山坡上，后来迁居山下。明景泰年间(1450—1456)渐成黟县一大都会。村庄东西长800米，南北宽300米，两条山溪自东而西穿村而过，村似船形。

西递代出名宦文人富商，人杰地灵。明清两代，实授官职者115人，廪生、贡生、监生多达298人。明代荆藩首相胡文光，清代巨贾胡贯三，其长子三品通议大夫胡尚熠、次子四品朝议大夫胡尚焘、三子正三品杭州知府胡元熙，其孙大收藏家胡积堂等高官富商文人为西递村带来了数百年的繁荣。清乾嘉年间，西递村鼎盛时期，全村曾有600余幢民宅，99条巷子，90余口水井，34幢祠堂，13座牌坊，5000人丁，何其昌盛!

历经数百年风雨，全村至今尚存古宅200余幢，以清初建筑居多，保存完整。古宅大多有人居住，人丁兴旺，古街巷韵味古朴，牌坊、祠堂雄风依存，山清水秀，鳞次栉比，堪称"徽派民居博物馆"。2000年11月，西递登录联合国《世界遗产名录》。

Hongcun and Xidicun – World cultural heritage

Hongcun

Hongcun is located in northwestern Yixian County. In 1131, 1st year of the Shaoxing reign of the Southern Song, the home of a Wang family at Qishucun was burned down by the fire of war, and as a result, Wang Yanji, 66th ancestor of the Wang family, moved south of Leigang Hill, and after 20 years of path-breaking efforts, built a house complex of thirteen rooms, and named the village Hongcun. In 1737, 2nd year of the reign of Emperor Qianlong, the village was homophonically renamed to avoid the same character in Emperor Qianlong's name. In the Yongle reign of the Ming (1403-1424), Wang Siqi, 76th ancestor of the Wang family, and his wife Hu Zhong, led to dig a canal to introduce water from the Xixi, to dig the Crescent Pool, and to build the ancestral house. Members of the clan came downhill to build new houses. In 1607, 35th year of the Wanli reign of the Ming, Wang Kuiguang, 81st ancestor of the Wang family, and sixteen others, led to dig South Lake, 20 247 sq m, south of the village, a project that took three full years. In the reigns of Emperors Qianlong and Jiajing of the Qing, the village grew into a "metropolis" of Yixian County. The village is buffalo-shaped.

The most colorful sights of Hongcun are the old water system, and the renowned Chengzhitang House. The canal carries clear spring water to every household, for the purposes of firefight, washing and irrigation. The Crescent Pool in the middle of the village, surrounded by old houses, looks dainty and can be viewed as the best sight of Hongcun. South Lake runs from east to west, encircled by old trees, and old houses on the north. The path and bridges, and great stretches of lotuses, create a poetic picture. The Chengzhitang House, located in the west of the village, with an area of more than 3 000 sq m, has spacious halls and side-halls. Notably, the woodcut paintings on the beams, doors and windows of the house present perfect skill and lively figures. These paintings are well-preserved, and are treated as a folk Summer Palace.

Hongcun has green Leigang Hill on the north, and the wavy South Lake on the south. At the entrance to the village stand old trees such as red poplars and ginkgoes, and in the middle of the village run the clear Crescent Pool and canal, and stand rows upon rows of old houses. Hongcun is indeed a paradise of water and sight. In November 2000, Hongcun entered *Directory of World Cultural Heritage*.

Hongcun has produced many talents in its history. In the Qing Dynasty, men of letters such as Wang Shitong and his son Wang Wenxue, Wang Chengen and his son Wang Tongwen, Wang Fangzhong, Wang Yiwen, as well as women authors Wang Fen and Qian Yan, left behind poetry and other literary works. In the Qing, Wang Zhaoyan and his brother Wang Zhaozhang, served as grand master for forthright service, and in the Republic of China, Wang Daxie, served as Acting Prime Minister, Prime Minister and Minister of Finance. These officials achieved political deeds and brought honor to their hometown. Famous merchants included Wang Shengping of the Ming, Wang Shoujia and his brother Wang Jiaju of the Qing, and Wang Dinggui of the late Qing, who contributed handsomely to the public architecture of villages, and left behind such houses as South Lake House, the Sanlitang House and the Chengzhitang House.

Xidicun

Xidicun, formerly Xichuan, situated west of the former Huizhou Prefecture, was so named for the postal service station Pu-di-suo, eight kilometers away from the county seat. The earliest ancestor of Xidicun was the son of Li Ye, Emperor Zhaozong of the Tang Dynasty, and because of war, was brought here by Hu San, resident of Kaochuan of Wuyuan County. He took the surname of Hu, and was given the first name Changyi. At the age of 22, Changyi passed the Imperial Examinations of Classics, and was later called "Ancestor Hu of Classics and Son of the Tang Emperor". In the Yuanfeng reign（1078-1085）of the Northern Song Dynasty, Hu Shiliang, 5th ancestor of the family, settled down on the hillside and then moved to the foot of the hill. In the Jingtai reign (1450-1456) of the Ming, Xidi grew into a metropolis of Yixian County. Xidicun extends for 800 meters from west to east, and 300 meters from north to south, and two streams run across the village from east to west. The village is boat-shaped.

Xidicun has produced many officials, men of letters and business talents. In the Ming and Qing, 115 Xidians took official posts, and 298 were either prefectural college students, tribute students, or Imperial College students. Hu Wenguang, Minister for the Lord of Jingzhou of the Ming, Hu Guansan, merchant of the Qing, his eldest son Hu Shangyi, who served as third-rank grand master for thorough counsel, his second son Hu Shangtao, who served as fourth-rank grand master for court discussions, his third son Hu Yuanxi, who served as third-rank prefect of Hangzhou, and his grandson Hu Jitang, collector, brought to Xidicun prosperity of several centuries. Xidicun reached its zenith in the reigns of Emperors Qianlong and Jiaqing of the Qing, when the village had more than 600 houses, 99 alleys, over 90 wells, 34 ancestral houses, 13 memorial archways, and 5 000 residents. What a picture of prosperity.

More than 200 old houses remain from the centuries of change. Many of them belong to architecture of the early Qing, and are preserved in good condition. Most are still in use, and large families live in them. The old streets and alleys radiate a dainty flavor, the archways and ancestral houses live in grandeur, creating a "house museum of Huizhou". In November 2000, Xidicun entered *Directory of Word Cultural Heritage*.

第一章
村庄环境与老房子结构
Chapter One
Village environment and the structure of old houses

在水一方石径斜（黟县屏山）
Stone path at waterside (Pingshan of Yixian County)

肥梁硕柱大券拱（宏村）
Large beam, column and arch（Hongcun）

第一节　引言

　　徽州位于长江以南，北纬30°，东经117°附近，年平均气温15℃—16℃，1月份极端低温−8℃—−10℃，7月份极端高温40℃—41℃，无霜期222—248天，年降水量1200—1700毫米，气候温暖，雨量丰富，年平均日照1800多小时，日照偏少，属于亚热带温润季风气候。徽州总面积12548平方公里，历史上耕地最多的年份（1578年）为169855公顷，占总面积的13.536%，山多田少，大大小小的山间盆地遍布全区，平畈区广种水稻，山清水秀，蓝天白云，小桥流水，白墙黑瓦的村舍散落在青山绿水之间，跨进徽州地界，一幅世外桃源般的田园风光，令八方来客赞誉不已。

　　徽州山多林茂，盛产杉、松、柏、枫、梓、银杏等优质林木，巨树比比皆是，山多地少，宅基地紧缺，乡村里多采山间巨木，建造二层、三层的砖木结构的楼房，不建平房，节省土地。

　　徽州人建房兴村，非常讲究风水环境。村庄选址要求背山面水，山环水抱，藏风聚气，子孙发达，村庄兴旺。尤其是村庄的水资源必须稳定丰富，水象征财富，水旺财气旺，活水能给村庄带来灵气，带来生活的便利。六百年前的宏村人，先挖水圳，掘月沼，引来山溪水，后建房子，用活水来打造家园，为子孙后代留下了一座户户方便、处处水景的美丽家园。

徽州的老房子的建筑结构，经历了几百年几十代人的总结改进，房子的结构样式已经成熟定型，几个十分显著的建筑特点，成了徽派民居的标本符号。

一是墙高、窗小、山墙砌成马头墙。徽州男人都在外经商，为防盗贼，保一家老小的平安，房子的墙高7—8米，围墙高4—5米，楼房的底层不开窗户，二楼才开一个高34厘米，宽30厘米的小窗户，夜里大门闩上，家里还是很安全的。房子两侧的山墙，都砌成高过屋脊的封火墙，以防火灾在邻居间蔓延，封火墙成阶梯形，高耸似马头，俗称马头墙，幢幢房子连成片，高低成阵的马头墙，酷似万马奔腾，气派非凡。

二是家有庭院。尽管徽州的地皮紧缺，大多数人家建房时都要在房前围建一处庭院，栽树养花，挖鱼塘，建水榭，夏夜乘凉，冬日晒太阳，确是一处修身养性的好地方。庭院内通厅堂，外接街巷，厅堂与庭院的空气对流，吐故纳新，庭院的空气比街巷的空气要新鲜、干净，家居环境也好得多。庭院还起着玄关的作用，路上行人一眼看不见厅堂里人的活动。所以，庭院是徽州民居的重要配置。

三是家家有天井。徽州老房子的墙高窗小，室内通风采光全靠天井，进进厅堂都有天井，天井在堂前，厅堂都是敞开式。徽州人将天井称作明堂，俗话说：四水归明堂（四周屋顶的雨水都流向天井），肥水不流外人田，水象征财富嘛。

老房子的天井还有一种独特的情趣，大门一关，高墙围起一小块天空就在屋里堂前，日月星辰、风雨雪雹都伴随着家人。大雪天，鹅毛大雪从天井簇拥而下，关上大门，一家老小坐火桶烫火锅饮酒赏雪，雪助酒兴，那个兴致岂不妙哉！

四是老房子讲究门口的朝向。大多数房子的大门口朝南或者朝东，朝西朝北的门口很少。朝向并非正南正东，一般都要偏10°—30°，冬暖夏凉，宜人居住。门口的前方尽量避开交叉的巷道、墙角、墙头、烟囱、窄弄、山头等不吉利的障碍物，难以避开时，可以在门楣上悬挂镜子、剪刀、八卦之类物件辟邪，也可以将门口偏转一个方向，或者在门前砌屏墙来辟邪，还可以在门口的墙上嵌入刻有"泰山石敢当"、"山镇海"文字的石块以辟邪。徽州有一句古话：千斤门楼四两屋。指的就是门口朝向的重要，门口处置不好，房子住人不顺利不吉利，门口的风水是很重要的，确定一个好门向，是徽州人建房子的头等大事。

五是对称的室内设置。中间厅堂两侧厢房的三间屋结构，是徽州老房子的基本结构。前后三间，四合屋等各种结构，都是多个三间屋组合而成，各种房型都强调前后，左右对称，整个房子就是一个稳定的结构，象征家庭的和睦稳定。

明末清初，十七世纪初，徽州的三间屋结构出现了一种改进型结构——廊步三间。它的不同之处，是厅堂靠天井的大梁（俗称：冬瓜梁），比厅堂上的大梁抬高了50厘米左右，目的是让天井的光线能够照射到厅堂最里边，加大了厅

春天的老屋
Old houses in spring

堂的进深，相适应也要加宽加高了厅堂，整个厅堂就更宽敞了。所以，稍有财力的人家都要建造"廊步三间"格式，形成了大厅堂小卧室的格局，房间小、暖和，厅堂大、气派，主人很体面。

宏村大户人家的名宅"承志堂"，占地2000多平方米，它的布局是以前、后厅为中轴线，两侧设置偏厅、书房、鱼塘厅、厨房、花园等辅助建筑，对称而平衡，稳重而不失灵气，功能齐全，装饰华丽，配置得当，确是一幢宜人居住的豪宅。

徽州古村落的老房子布局，也很有讲究。祠堂、庙宇是村民祭祀祖先、神灵的地方，房子也特别高大，是村庄的公共活动中心，亦好比是村庄的重器，它们一般都建在村中的龙脉之上，龙脉就是村庄的少祖山（来龙山）的主脉山势在村中的延长线，祠堂、庙宇建在龙脉上，也消受得起龙脉之气，村庄才会人丁兴旺。书院私塾建在村中幽静之处，街道纵横村中，民宅则散布全村。这样，村民从卧室（私密空间）到厅堂（俗话说：房内夫妻，堂上君子，内外有别，男女授受不亲），再到庭院，从庭院到街巷、祠堂、庙宇、书院等公共空间，再到村外道路田野。民宅、公共建筑、村庄、田野，从小空间到大空间，从家庭小圈子到社会的大圈子，构成了一幅社会伦礼道德的建筑文化图景，也是一幅人与社会，人与自然和谐相处的乡村画卷，徽州的青山绿水，古村老屋，留存到今天，也把这幅朴拙平实、美丽生动的乡村画卷留存到今天，留存给未来。

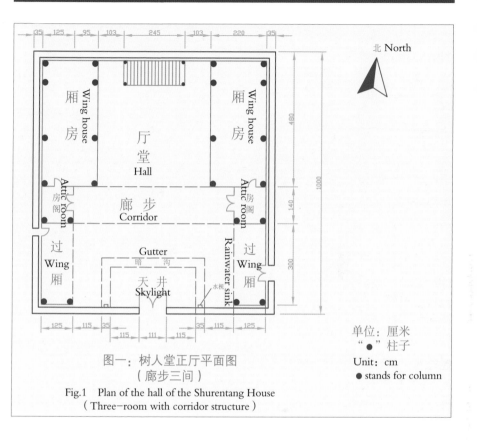

图一：树人堂正厅平面图
（廊步三间）
Fig.1　Plan of the hall of the Shurentang House
（Three-room with corridor structure）

1.1　Introduction

Huizhou, situated south of the Yangtze, 30 degrees north latitude and 117 degrees east longitude, belongs to a subtropical warm monsoon climate. It has an annual mean temperature of 15℃~16℃. The lowest temperatures in January are −8℃~−10℃, and the highest temperatures in July are 40℃ ~41℃. The no-frost period is 222~248 days, and the annual precipitation is 1 200~1 700mm. It is warm, with a rich rainfall and an annual average sunshine time of more than 1 800 hours, on the short side. Huizhou covers an area of 12 548 sq km, with 169 855 hectares of farming land in 1578, which covered 13.536% of the total area. It is hilly, and hilly basins of various sizes spread over. The plain section is full of paddy fields, green hills and clear water, blue

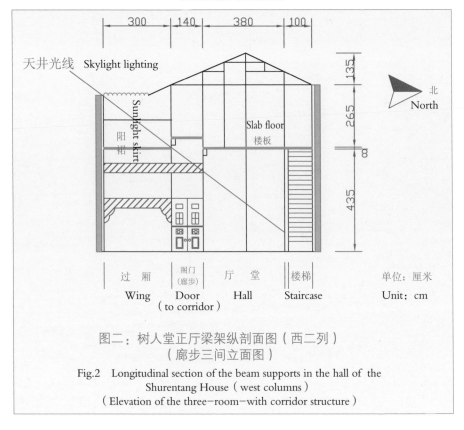

天井光线 Skylight lighting

Sunlight skirt

阳裙

Slab floor
楼板

北
North

| 过 厢 | 阁门（廊步） | 厅 堂 | 楼梯 | 单位：厘米 |
| Wing | Door (to corridor) | Hall | Staircase | Unit：cm |

图二：树人堂正厅梁架纵剖面图（西二列）
（廊步三间立面图）

Fig.2　Longitudinal section of the beam supports in the hall of the
Shurentang House（west columns）
（Elevation of the three－room－with corridor structure）

sky and white clouds, as well as rivers and bridges. Houses of white walls and dark tiles are scattered in between. At the sight of Huizhou, tourists see a pastoral landscape of a Shangri－la and cannot help adoring it.

Huizhou is hilly and grovy, and produces firs, pines, cypresses, maples, catalpas, gingkoes, and so forth, many of which are tall. As the area is hilly, house sites are scarce, many use wood from huge trees, and two－ or three－story brick and wood buildings, rather than bungalows, are constructed to save land.

Huizhouans give much care to *fengshui* when they build houses and villages. The site of a village requires hill and water. The embrace of hill and water means the accumulation of *qi*, which in turn means many offspring and a prosperous village. The water resources must be rich and steady, because water symbolizes wealth, and running water brings soul and comfortable life to a village. The residents of Hongcun living six centuries ago dug a canal and the Crescent Pool to lead stream water before they began to build houses. The running water helped to create beautiful homes for their descendants, where convenience and water sights were characteristic.

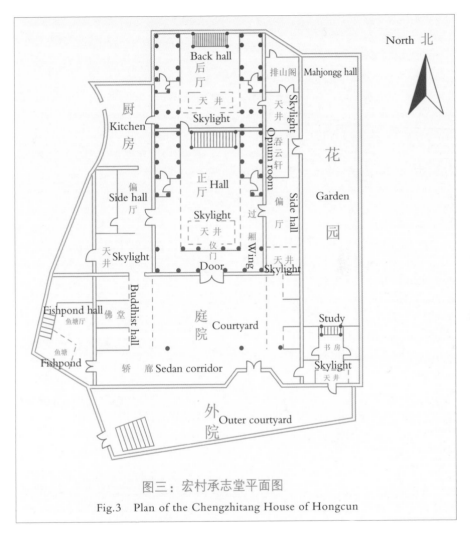

图三：宏村承志堂平面图

Fig.3　Plan of the Chengzhitang House of Hongcun

The patterns of the structure of old houses of Huizhou, after centuries of improvement, have taken full shape. Several architectural features have become the labels of Huizhou-style houses:

First, the houses have tall walls and small windows, and the horse-head wall acts as the gable of each house. Men of Huizhou do business away from their hometown, and to prevent burglary and provide security to their families, they come up with walls of 7~8 m high and enclosed walls of 4~5 m high. The ground floor has no windows, and even the second floor has only small windows, generally 34 cm × 30 cm. At night, when the door is bolted, families find security inside. The gable walls are built into fireproof walls, in case that fires spread to neighboring houses. A fire wall, step—shaped and tall like a horse—head, is informally termed as a horse—head wall. In this way, rows upon rows of houses, and horse—head walls of varying heights, radiate grandeur of horses running in great herds.

Second, each house has a courtyard. Though house sites are scarce, many families enclose a courtyard in front of their houses, in which they grow flowers, dig fishponds, and construct water pavilions. Here, families get cool shades in summer, and sit for sunlight in winter; the courtyard is ideal for health care. The courtyard leads to the hall, and looks on the street or alley, so that new air keeps coming in, and that the air in the courtyard is fresher than that on the street or alley, bringing in a better living environment. The courtyard also gives privacy: pedestrians can hardly see the activity in the hall. In other words, the courtyard is a major setting of a Huizhou house.

Third, each house has a skylight. As the old houses of Huizhou have tall walls and small windows, ventilation and lighting depend solely on their skylights. Each hall has a skylight, in the front of an open hall. Residents call their skylights *mingtang* (bright hall), evidently in response to the proverb: Water in four directions comes to the bright hall. Water, a symbol of wealth, shall never go elsewhere.

The skylight of an old house has special appeal: when the door is locked, the tall wall creates a small patch of sky for the whole family, where they are accompanied by the sun, the moon and stars, and winds, rain, snow and hail. In heavy snowfall, snowflakes crowd in through the skylight, and the whole family drinks and enjoys the snow by sitting around the hot pot. Snow adds zest to the drinking, and this is the wish of every single soul!

Fourth, each house emphasizes its direction. The doorways of most houses face south or east, while those of only a few face west or north. Of course the directions are not straight south or straight east, but usually 10° to 30° degrees from either direction. The house is warm in winter and cool in summer. Ahead of the doorways, there must be as few crossing streets, corners, walls, chimneys, narrow alleys or other objects of ill luck as possible. Where impossible, mirrors, scissors or other objects can be hung to avoid evil spirits, or a site more degrees from the direction is chosen for the doorway, or a screen wall is built to dispel evil spirits, or stones inscribed with "this stone can drive Mount Taishan away" and so on are embedded in the wall to dispel the evil. As a local proverb goes, "arch gates weigh a thousand kilograms while the house itself weighs only half a kilogram", referring to the importance of the direction that a house faces, because when the house faces the wrong direction, its residents will meet misfortune or ill luck. A good direction, therefore, is essential to the construction of a house.

Finally, each house has a symmetrical

design. The three—room structure, in which the hall has a wing on both sides, is the basic structure of an old Huizhou house. The three—room structures in front and at the back, as well as the courtyard houses, are multiple three—room constructions. All the patterns emphasize symmetry, and the entire house is a steady structure, symbolizing the harmony of a family.

In the late Ming and early Qing, an improved structure, i.e., the three—room—with—corridor pattern, occurred. It differed from the earlier pattern in that the beam of the skylight next to the hall ("white—gourd beam") was raised approximately 50 cm above the beam of the hall, for the purpose that the lighting from the skylight could come into the innermost section of the hall, and thus expand the depth of the hall. Correspondingly, the hall was expanded in width and height, so that it looked more spacious. For that reason, a family of decent wealth would follow the new pattern, to create large halls and small bedrooms. A small bedroom provided greater warmth, and a large hall offered grandeur and decency to the owner of the house.

The Chengzhitang House covers an area of more than 2 000 sq m. The house takes the front and back halls as the axis, with a side hall, a study, a fishpond hall, a kitchen, a garden and other auxiliaries at the sides. This pattern offers symmetry and balance, steadiness and vigor, with full functions, elaborate decorations, and proper settings, and indeed creates a comfortable house.

The other old houses are also noted for their layout. The ancestral house and the temple, where villagers offer sacrifices to their ancestors and gods, are large and tall. They are the center of public activities. As the highlight of the village, they are usually built in the "dragon vein" of the village. The dragon vein is the extension of Shaozu (or Lailong) Hill in the village. The ancestral house and the temple built along the dragon vein absorb its vigor and symbolize the productivity of offspring. The private school is constructed in a quiet section, streets run across, and houses spread over. The bedroom (private space), the hall (as the proverb goes, man and wife in the private space, gentlemen and friends in the hall, that makes the difference), public space such as the courtyard, the streets and alleys, the ancestral house and the temple, and the school, and then the roads and fields outside the village — the houses, public architecture, the village and the fields go from small space to large space, from the family circle to the societal circle, and create a picture of architectural culture embedding social ethics and morality and a scroll of a village where man and nature exist in harmony. This scroll of simplicity, beauty and liveliness is preserved to today, and to the future, along with the green hills and blue water of Huizhou, and with the old houses.

水口古桥（黟县南屏）
Old bridge at the water entry (Nanping of Yixian County)

第二节　山水田园风光

徽州古村倚水而居，在小溪的下游，离村数百米的地方，称作古村的水口，进了水口，即到了一村的地界。水口是村庄的屏障，与房子的玄关相似。村民在水口处栽树、建庙、筑亭、架桥，成了一处古树参天，小桥流水，亭阁迎客的水口园林景观，亦是村庄的风水宝地。

1.2　Pastoral landscape

The old villages of Huizhou are surrounded by water, and stand in the lower reaches of streams. Several hundred meters from a village there is the water entry to the village. When one arrives at the water entry, he is said to be at the village boundary. The water entry acts as the screen for the village, similar to the hallway in a house. Here, villagers plant trees, build a temple, construct a pavilion, and/or set up a bridge. It provides a landscape of a water entry garden where ancient trees, small bridges and a welcoming pavilion exist, and is thus the treasure section of a village.

歙县唐模村水口亭
Water Entry Pavilion at Tangmocun of Yixian County

老房子层层叠叠（西递村）
Rows upon rows of old houses (Xidicun)

石碣头的风情（宏村）
Stone stairs（Hongcun）

深秋的靓丽
Beauty of high autumn

油菜花海里的卢村
Lucun in rape flowers

红叶深处有人家
A village hidden deep in red leaves

塔川村的水口古樟
Old camphor at the water entry to Tachuancun

第三节　巷弄

古村巷弄纵横交错，曲折迷离，或上或下，或窄或宽，变化莫测，家家门前巷子深。巷口弄尾弯曲处，拱形门洞跨巷而立，丰富了巷弄的层次感，增加了空间视觉的美感。

纵横交错（宏村）
Intertwined（Hongcun）

1.3 Alleys

Alleys of an old village are intertwined in a zigzag. They are raised or lowered, narrow or wide, creating an unpredictable pattern; a deep alley leads to the doorway of every household. The corner of an alley, with an arch overhead, enriches the layering of alleys and creates esthetic appeal of spatial vision.

深邃曲长（南屏）
Profound and long（Nanping）

沧桑岁月（塔川）
Vicissitudes（Tachuan）

昔日的辉煌（屏山）
Past glory（Pingshan）

巷里春早（南屏）
Early spring at alley（Nanping）

步步高（西递）
Ascending step by step (Xidicun)

第四节　马头墙

　　徽州居民两侧的山墙，都砌成阶梯式高于屋脊的封火墙，失火不易波及邻居。封火墙似马头形，俗称"马头墙"，高低错落，万马奔腾，蔚为壮观。

似马奔腾，似琴低吟（屏山）
Like running horses, like low-playing lutes（Pingshan）

1.4 Horse–head walls

The gable walls are built into fireproof walls that are stepped above the ridge, so that a fire will not easily spread to neighboring houses. As fireproof walls look like horse-heads, they are popularly termed "horse-head walls", which create grandeur out of the intertwining, very much like thousands of running horses.

古村里的靓丽（宏村月沼）
Beauty in the old village（Crescent Pool , Hongcun）

老墙头的春光（宏村）
Spring at old wall（Hongcun）

舒缓的马头墙（南屏）
Gentle horse-head walls（Nanping）

黑白交错，气象万千（宏村）
Black and white intertwined（Hongcun）

寂静的古宅（宏村）
Quiet old houses（Hongcun）

天际轮廓线（西递）
Horizon（Xidicun）

密集的马头墙（西递）
Densely-populated horse-head walls（Xidicun）

第五节　门口与门楼

　　徽州人造房子，非常重视大门口的朝向，关乎房子住人的凶吉。徽州人常常用斜门口、挂镜子、砌屏墙、埋"泰山石敢当"镇石等方式辟邪。房子的大门口砌成高大精美的砖雕门楼，显示家族的兴旺和荣耀。

屏山祠堂的大门楼
Large archway to Pingshan Ancestral House

"门不直冲巷",在门侧墙角立碑石"泰山石敢
当",以避邪气。
The tablet stone inscribed with "this stone can drive
Mount Taishan away" is meant to dispel evil spirits.

1.5 Doorways and arch gates

Huizhouans emphasize the direction of the doorway, which is believed to be critical to the luck of the residents of a house. They often protect themselves from evil spirits by building a slant doorway, hanging a mirror, laying a screen wall, or burying an evil-dispelling stone. Above the doorway a tall and elaborate brick carving arch gate is constructed, a structure that symbolizes the prosperity and glory of a family.

耳门外斜内正，调整了朝向
The outer slant and inner straight of the ear door adjusts
the direction

八字门楼
Archway shaped like the character "eight"

叶门
Leaf door

大门口的屏墙，遮住了对面的山头，避了冲气。
Screen wall at the doorway hides the hill beyond and thus avoids ill luck.

三间四柱五楼式大门楼（西递）
Three-room four-column five-story archway
（Xidicun）

官宦人家大门口的下马石
Horse-mount stone at the doorway to an official's household

官厅的门楼（西递）
Archway to the official's hall（Xidicun）

天井下的内门楼，遮住了门，又多了一点美。（宏村）
Inner archway under the skylight hides the door and adds beauty.（Hongcun）

八字门楼的气派（关麓）
Fashion of archway shaped like the character "eight"（Guanlu）

东园门楼（西递）
Archway to East Garden（Xidicun）

第六节　庭院与水榭

　　尽管徽州的地皮珍贵，徽州人家还要在房子外圈起围墙，建座庭院，栽树养花，假山鱼池，亭阁水榭，晾晒衣物，夏夜乘凉，冬日孵太阳，修身养性。院内空气新鲜，与室内空气对流，改善居住环境。隔着庭院，路人不易看见房子里的活动，又起到玄关的作用。

书房厅前的小庭院，幽静雅致（卢村）
Small courtyard in front of the study hall, quiet and refined（Lucun）

1.6 Courtyards and water pavilions

Though house sites are scarce, residents usually enclose an outer wall to create a courtyard, where they grow trees and flowers, build artificial rocks and fishponds, construct pavilions, hang clothing, and seek cool shade at summer night or sit for sunlight in winter for health care. The air in the courtyard is fresh, and flows with the air inside the house, thus improving the living environment. The courtyard acts as a hallway, so that passersby cannot easily see the activity in the house.

高墙下的大庭院（南屏）
Large courtyard inside the high wall (Nanping)

连扇的雕花门给庭院添色不少（卢村）
Carved folding door adds color to the courtyard（Lucun）

圆拱门前牡丹开，花好月圆（西递）
Peony flowers bloom in front of the round arch door: a picture of good flowers and a round moon（Xidicun）

桃园居的后花园，别有洞天（宏村）
Back garden at Taoyuanju creates a different taste（Hongcun）

古树奇石老屋，过日子的好地方（西递西园）
Old tree, rare stone and old house, where good days are never past（West Garden, Xidicun）

百年奇茶树，红花、白花共树生（卢村）
Century-old tea tree: red and white flowers grow in the same tree（Lucun）

书屋庭院（关麓）
Courtyard to the study hall（Guanlu）

古今中外的温馨，天性和谐（宏村德义堂）
Natural harmony from warmth in all directions
（Deyitang House, Hongcun）

引水入院，水榭会友，福地自有惜福人家（宏村碧园）
Leading water to the courtyard and meeting friends at the water
pavilion: a happiness-cherishing family lives in a place of happiness
（Biyuan Garden, Hongcun）

精美的装饰背后，是精致的生活（宏村剑琴榭）
Behind elegant decorations is elegant life（Jianqinxie
Pavilion, Hongcun）

第七节　天井

　　徽州人家的房子里都有大小不一的天井，日月星辰，春雨冬雪，皆到堂前，天人合一。水枧接雨水，四水归明塘，水主财，暗含"肥水不流外人田"之意。

天井下的居家日子（歙县雄村）
Life under the skylight（Xiongcun of Xixian County）

1.7 Skylights

The houses of Huizhou each have skylights, of varying sizes, so that the sun, moon and stars, as well as rain and snow, come into the house, creating a picture of harmony between man and heaven. The rainwater sink receives rainwater, and water runs into the pond, implying that "Nourishing water shall never flow into the fields of others", as water symbolizes wealth.

小偏厅里的小天井（歙县许村）
Small skylight in a small side hall (Xucun of Xixian County)

天井宽一点，厅堂亮一点（西递）
The broader the skylight, the brighter the hall (Xidicun)

五开间的天井特别宽敞（宏村）
A skylight of a five-room structure is particularly spacious (Hongcun)

从窄窄的天井射下的阳光，给老屋带来了温暖（屏山）
Sunshine from the narrow skylight brings warmth to the old house（Pingshan）

小天井下是鱼塘，浑然天成（宏村承志堂）
Below the small skylight is a fishpond, a true natural sight（Chengzhitang House, Hongcun）

小厨房里的小天井（歙县许村）
Small skylight in a small kitchen（Xucun of Xixian County）

第八节 砖雕与石雕

徽州的砖雕，常常砌在门楼上，祥云、瑞兽，历史典故，神话传说等，都是砖雕的题材，镂空几层雕，画面布局自然流畅，人物刻画惟肖惟妙，是门楼上绝妙的装饰构件。

石雕，常用青石雕刻而成。石柱，石柱础，石门枋，石碑刻，石漏窗、石条屏、石鼓、石瓶、石佛、石桌、石凳、石镜等等石雕艺术品，千姿百态，玲珑剔透，徽州一绝。由于石雕作品造价高昂，一般用于祠堂、亭庙、牌坊以及大户人家的门窗装饰和摆设。

欢庆胜利（石雕）
Celebration of victory（Stone carving）

1.8 Brick and stone carvings

Brick carvings are often used in arch gates. Their themes include clouds, beasts, historical stories, mythology and legends. With the hollowed-out pattern, the natural and smooth layout and lively figures constitute perfect decorations on arch gates.

Stone carvings are often made from blue stone. Stone pillars, stone plinths, stone door-columns, stone tablets, stone windows, stone screens, stone drums, stone vases, stone buddhas, stone tables, stone stools, stone mirrors and so forth, in all postures and exquisitely wrought, are an exclusive of Huizhou. As stone carvings are costly, they are mostly used in ancestral houses, temples, memorial archways, and as door and window decorations in large households.

祝寿图（砖雕）
Celebrating birthday
（Brick carving）

光宗耀祖（砖雕）
Bringing honor to ancestors（Brick carving）

钓兴正浓（砖雕）
Fishing（Brick carving）

城头厮杀（石雕）
Fight on the wall（Stone carving）

薛仁贵征西（砖雕门楼）
Xue Rengui Conquers the West（Brick carving arch gate）

石瓶（1）
Stone vase（1）

石瓶（2）
Stone vase（2）

梅竹石窗
Plum and bamboo stone window

雕花圆形石窗
Carved stone window

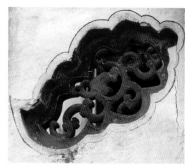

叶形石窗
Leaf-like stone window

松石石窗
Stone window of the pine and stone pattern

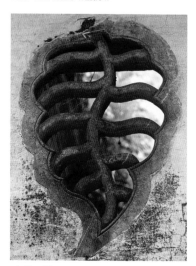

叶形石窗
Leaf-like stone window

寿字石窗
"Longevity" stone window

喜鹊登梅石窗
Stone window of the magpie-
in-the-plum pattern

金龙吐水石雕
Stone carving of the dragon-
puffs-out-water pattern

青石柱础
Blue stone plinth

石柱础
Stone plinth

石狮
Stone lion

石鼓
Stone drum

石镜
Stone mirror

石香炉
Stone incense burner

捆竹石凳
Bamboo-bound stone stool

石佛
Stone Buddha

第九节　厅堂、偏厅与过厢

　　徽州老房子的厅堂高大宽敞明亮，堂匾、中堂、楹联、条屏字画，书香人家比比皆是。东瓶西镜，条几八仙桌椅，摆放整齐，待人接物，清新雅致。厢房前的空间是过厢，内设边门进出，过厢内可起居置物。老屋多有偏厅书屋，小巧雅致，日常起居，尤其便当。

厅堂上对弈（南屏）
Chess play in the hall（Nanping）

1.9　Halls, side halls and wings

The halls of the old houses are tall, spacious and bright, and plaques, scrolls, scroll couplets and screen calligraphy or paintings are common in the halls of literary families. A vase on the east end and a mirror on the west end, a narrow table and a square table neatly prepared for guests, creating a fresh and refined atmosphere. The space in front of the wing house is the wing, installed with a side door and used as a living room. Most old houses have side halls and studies, which are petite and dainty, as well as convenient.

老家庭老摆设（西递）

Old furnishings in the old house（Xidicun）

绩溪县上庄村的胡适故居

Hu Shi's former residence in Shangzhuang of Jixi County

胡适（1891-1962 ）字适之。二十世纪中国新文化运动先驱，提倡白话文，尊重人权，反对独裁和文化专制。

Hu Shi (1891-1962), called Shi Zhi, was an avant-courier of Chinese New Culture Movement in 20th century. He advocated the vernacular Chinese and respected human rights; he opposed dictatorship and cultural despotism.

"大夫第"里过日子（西递）
Living in the "Minister's House"（Xidicun）

著名艺术家舒绣文故居（屏山）
Former residence of artist Shu Xiuwen（Pingshan）

充满现代气息的百年老屋（南屏）
Century-old house full of a modern taste（Nanping）

西递村高官的故居
Former residence of high official from Xidicun

秀气典雅的偏厅（屏山）
Lovely and refined side hall（Pingshan）

幽静的后厅（西递）
Quiet back hall（Xidicun）

带烟床的偏厅（关麓）
Side hall with a smoking bed（Guanlu）

带天窗的书房厅（关麓）
Study hall with a skylight window（Guanlu）

夜里佛堂静悄悄（承志堂）
Quiet Buddhist hall in the middle of night（Chengzhitang House）

玩麻将的"排山阁"（宏村）
Mahjongg hall（Hongcun）

木雕楼的过厢（卢村）
Wing of woodcut house（Lucun）

带庭院的书房厅（卢村）
Study hall with courtyard（Lucun）

装挂络的过厢（宏村）
Wing with hangings（Hongcun）

装雕花窗的过厢（西递）
Wing with carved window (Xidicun)

第十节　老厨房

徽州老房子的厨房建在主屋的一侧，受地基限制，不规则多边形的厨房比较多，二层楼砖木结构，屋内开天井采光通风，没有烟囱，长年烟熏后，墙壁梁柱上烟尘多，又黄又黑，光线又暗，大风天气，烟出不去，室内呛人。

炊烟袅袅的山村（婺源）
Village with heavy cooking smoke（Wuyuan County）

1.10　Old kitchens

The kitchens of old houses stand at one side of the main structure, and for the limitation of house sites, such kitchens are mostly irregular and polygonal. Each is a two-story structure, with a skylight for lighting and ventilation purposes. Without a chimney, and after years of smoking, the walls, beams and columns are smoky and dusty, yellow and dark, and have poor lighting. During gusty winds, the smoke cannot be dispelled, and is choky.

烟熏火燎老厨房（宏村）
Old kitchen with thick smoke（Hongcun）

老灶头（南屏）
Old kitchen range（Nanping）

第二章
老房子室内装饰风格

Chapter Two
Interior decorations of old houses

陶渊明送菊
Tao Yuanming sends chrysanthemums

有庆堂（屏山）
Youqingtang House（Pingshan）

第一节　引言

　　徽州老房子除了村里村外旖旎的田园风光和人文气息、独特的建筑结构以外，最突出的地方建筑特色就是朴拙和谐、清新雅致的室内装饰。

　　老房子的室内装饰由木雕与彩绘、楹联、堂匾与中堂，家具与摆设三个部分组成，大量使用图画、书法和诗文来表现视觉艺术和文学内涵，突出"仁、义、礼、智、信"，"忠、贞、节、孝、勇"的儒家思想，充分利用室内梁柱、门窗、板壁、天花板、地面等各个立面，巧妙构思，精心布局。工匠必求高手，图文务须精致，竭力营造一个朴拙而不繁复、精致而不纤弱的家居文化环境。

　　老房子室内所有的木雕、彩绘、书法、图画、家具等等都是明清时代徽商鼎盛时期产生的独特风格的地方艺术品集合。徽商贾而好儒，崇文识礼。徽州建筑文化是当时徽州社会自然产生的一种艺术时尚，并在当时社会上普遍较高的艺术审美水准的催生下，产生了成千上万的高层次的艺术精品。离开了特定的社会文化环境，离开了高墙天井、木梁木柱的老房子，离开了富商强大的文化需求，离开了师徒相传、高手如云、日益成熟的雕匠行业，现代的仿造和复制，必定缺失文化传承的神韵，最终只是支离破碎的艺术拾遗。

　　木雕图案是老房子室内装饰的主体配置。清朝后期，徽州室内木雕覆及老房子的月梁、额枋、斗拱、雀替、斜撑、挂络、莲花门、窗栏板等各类建筑构件；

带天井的回廊偏厅（宏村承志堂）
Corridor side hall with skylight（Chengzhitang
House, Hongcun）

八仙桌、条几、木椅、书桌、衣柜等各式家具，以柏、梓、椿、楠、枫、白果等优质木料为基质，雕刻工艺集汇了深浅浮雕、圆雕、透雕、凹雕、线刻、多层雕等各种技法。已经十分成熟的徽州雕版印刷技术，成了木雕艺术传承演化的行业基础。山石、树木采用遒劲的涩刀技法，给人以粗犷沉雄、苍劲古拙的美感；人物楼阁、行云流水，采用轻捷的切刀技术，给人以细腻明快、挺劲秀丽的印象。两种刻法均源自徽州版画，巧妙组合，画面更富有层次感。

一幢房子的木雕图案的整体设计，要求构思严谨，前后呼应，题材新颖，画面生动，大小适配，总体和谐。总体设计和各个部件单个画面的设计，是木雕成功的基础，需要房主与工匠的默契配合，既要遵照主人的意愿和财力的大小，又要充分发挥工匠高超的技艺和大胆创新的潜力。看起来房主的意愿是首要的，实际上工匠的技艺才是真正的关键。无论是构图和雕刻，工匠的专业水准的高低，决定了木雕图案的艺术水平，而房主的艺术审视的眼光，促使工匠在同行激烈的竞争中不断创新出个性鲜明、别具一格的艺术精品来。

老房子里的木雕图案的题材，主要来源于民间流传的历史典故和传统故事，比如"二十四孝"、"忠孝节义"、"八仙过海"、"读书及第"、"福禄寿"等等反映儒家礼教、道家风骨、佛家教义的各类题材，突出反映主人的吉祥如意、家业兴旺的美好愿望。有的是直观的场景，有的是取动植物的谐音，有的粗犷、有的细腻，有的简约、有的缜密。在色彩的运用上，大多不施油漆，显示木质的原色之美，少数部位才用金色，显得富贵堂皇。

清朝中后期，老房子流行起在天花板上彩绘图画的时尚。彩绘常用的素材是牡丹、菊花、兰花、石榴、葡萄、蝴蝶、仕女等寓意吉祥的动植物和人物，用靛青、铅黄、朱砂之类的耐久鲜艳的天然颜料，画匠在杉木拼板上精心描绘而成。画面非常细腻逼真，布局严谨，漂亮的静物画中蕴含着生命的律动，增加了仰视空间的美感，少了顶棚的空白，整个室内的艺术层次也丰富得多。

徽州大户人家的正厅都有个堂名，称"堂"者多。祠堂、书院亦有堂名，也有人家称"居"、"轩"、"庭"者。堂名既可作为房子的标识，又显雅致，寄托着主人对后人的期望。堂匾常请名家书写，大楷字体居多，进门抬头一看很有气势。堂匾下面悬挂中堂。山水图画，楷书"朱子治家格言"都是常见的中堂，东西两侧挂四条屏字画者亦多。而厅堂的柱子上悬挂木制抱柱楹联，几乎是老房子装饰的必备要件。朱砂底金字、淡灰底石绿字、黑底金字、赭底黑字等各种用色都是楹联的流行做法。名家书法，正草隶篆，皆有功力。联文对仗工整，琅琅上口，直白易懂，富含处世做人的哲理，既可欣赏书法艺术，又可咀嚼个中文化的真谛，也成了传世的家训。

老房子室内的木雕、堂匾、中堂、楹联，都是主人精力和财力的积累，每一件都是传世的艺术品，也是主人十分看重的家族精神依托，倍加珍惜。累世传承，也成了今天越来越少的珍贵文物。

老房子厅堂上的家具摆设也很讲究。厅正中自里而外，长条几，八仙桌，桌子两侧是木椅，厅堂两侧摆放茶几和木椅，八仙桌两侧是主人和贵宾的座位，两侧待客用。特别有趣的是长条几上的陈设，东边大花瓶，西侧座镜，中

莲花门窗（宏村）
Lotus door and window（Hongcun）

间一台自鸣钟，男左女右，男人外出经商，平平（瓶）安安，女人在家心静（镜）如水，钟声响起，钟声、瓶、镜，寓意"终身平静，一生平安"。由于自鸣钟是19世纪后期传入中国，这种说法应该是晚清的事情。钟的两侧摆两只帽筒，有人说是男人扣瓜皮小帽的，有人说帽筒里插放引火用的纸媒，寓意香火茂盛，谐音"帽筒"，都有点道理。正厅的厢房是主人的卧室，也是儿子成婚的新房。房间很小，雕花床、马鞍桌、骨牌凳、衣橱、马桶等等家具摆得满满的，显得有点挤，但是，窝小也很暖和。

木雕和彩绘，堂匾、中堂和楹联，家具摆设，三大要素构成了徽派民居室内装饰的独特风格，朴拙中见其功力深厚，含蓄里映现文化渊源，环视里外上下左右，既非梁柱隔板平铺直装的无趣，也少见华而不实的虚浮堆砌，朴实无华的木雕字画，带给您吉祥的祝福，也带给您和谐的美感享受。

老房子，远去的家。

招财进宝（木俑）
Bringing in wealth and treasure（wooden figures）

红叶里的村庄
Village in red leaves

2.1 Introduction

Apart from the pastoral landscape outside the village, and the unique structure of houses with a rich cultural atmosphere, the most evident feature of old houses of Huizhou is their interior decorations of harmonious simplicity which are fresh and refined.

The interior decorations are composed of three parts: woodcuts and color paintings; scroll couplets, plaques and scrolls; and furniture and furnishings. Drawings, calligraphy and poetry are extensively used to exhibit visual art and literary connotations, to emphasize the Confucian ideology of "benevolence, righteousness, propriety, wisdom and faithfulness"and "loyalty, uprightness, integrity, filial piety and bravery". Beams and columns, doors and windows, walls, ceilings and floors are fully utilized for perfect conception and layout. Skilled artisans are sought for the purpose, and drawings and poetry must be refined, to create a cultural atmosphere that is simple but not redundant, that is refined but not slight.

All the woodcuts, color paintings, calligraphy, drawings and furniture are collections of unique local works of art that are produced in the prime of Huizhou merchants of the Ming and Qing dynasties. Huizhou merchants do business but at the same time are literary. The architectural culture was an artistic fashion derived from society and nature, which, under the influence of high standards of artistic esthetics, produced millions of sophisticated works of art. With the special socio—cultural atmosphere, with the old houses of high walls, skylights, and wooden beams and columns, with the cultural needs of the rich merchants, without the sophisticated carving industry in which old hands gather and master—disciple skill inheritance dominates, imitation and duplication in modern times will be short of the spirit of cultural heritage and the result will be broken pieces of art.

The patterns of woodcuts make the major settings of interior decorations. In the late Qing, the carvings were used on crescent beams, horizontal tablets, bucket arches, sparrow braces, hangings, lotus doors, and window boards; on square tables, narrow tables, wooden chairs, desks, and closets, which take cypress, Chinese catalpa, Chinese toon, camphor, maple and gingko wood. The art of carving collected deep and shallow relief, round carving, fretwork, hollow relief, line carving, multi—layer carving, and so forth. The carving printing of Huizhou became the basis for the inheritance and evolution of woodcuts. The vigorous hard—knife technique was used on mountain stone and wood, in order to produce a rough and bold esthetic sense; the swift cut—knife technique was used on figures, pavilions, clouds and water, in order to create a fine and swift impression. Both techniques derived from Huizhou woodcuts, and when combined, produced richer layering.

The overall design of woodcut patterns of a house requires rigorous conception, consistency, thematic novelty, liveliness, sizing and overall harmony. The overall design and that of individual pieces form the basis for the success of a piece of woodcut, and requires the close cooperation between the house owner and the artisans. They have to fulfill the wishes and wealth of the owner, and to display the artisanship and creativity of the artisans. The wishes of the owner seem to be of paramount importance, but actually the ingenuity of the artisan is the key. Whether in terms of design or carving, the level of proficiency of the artisans determines the artistic level of the woodcut patterns. Of course, the insight of the owner encourages the constant creation of unique works of art in the fierce competition among artisans.

The themes of the woodcut patterns come from folk legends and traditional stories, such as "Twenty—four Pious Sons", "Loyalty, filial piety, righteousness and integrity", "The Eight Immortals Cross the Seas", "Good students make good officials", "Happiness, fortune and longevity", and other themes that reflect Confucian etiquette, Daoist vigor and Buddhist doctrines and the good wishes for good fortune and a prosperous family. Some are actual scenes, and some take the homophones of animals or plants. Some are of a rough style and some are of a delicate style. Some emphasize simplicity, and some stress density. In the use of colors, paint is seldom applied, in order to retain the original color of the wood; only at some points is gold used to show nobility and grandeur.

In the mid- and late Qing, color paintings on ceilings began its popularity. Peonies, chrysanthemums, orchids, pomegranates, grapes, butterflies, and ladies, which are symbols of good luck, are commonly used. Lasting and bright-colored natural paints such as indigo, lead oxide and cinnabar are applied by the painters who work with great caution on fir ceilings. The paintings are fine and lively, the layout rigorous, and the beautiful still figures revealing dynamic life, which improve the esthetics of the look-up space. Without the emptiness of the ceiling, the interior decorations unveil a richer atmosphere.

The hall of a large household has a name, and the character "tang" is commonly used. The halls of ancestral houses and public school also have names, some of which use the characters "ju", "xuan" and "ting". The names serve

as the symbol of a house and show elegance, reflecting the expectations of the owner for his descendants. The plaques often take the works of well-known calligraphers, most of the regular script, which sends out a feeling of magnificence. Below the plaque hang the scrolls. Landscape paintings,

残缺的美
Dilapidated beauty

combined with classic sayings in regular script, are common scrolls, on the sides of which hangs calligraphy. On the columns of the hall hang column—stuck scroll couplets, which is almost a necessity in an old house. Various colors for the calligraphy, such as gold characters with cinnabar ground, stone green characters with pale gray ground, gold characters with black ground, and black characters with reddish brown ground, are common practice with scroll couplets. The calligraphy, of the regular, cursive, official or seal scripts, radiate profundity. The couplets are balanced and rhymed for reading aloud, and send messages of moral behavior. These couplets serve not only as art, but also as the carrier of truth that can be handed down as family sayings.

The woodcuts, plaques, scrolls and scroll couplets, in a sense, are collections of the energy and wealth of their owner. Each piece is a work of art and constitutes the spiritual support of the clan that its owner cherishes. Handed down over the generations, these works of art become precious relics.

The furniture and furnishings in the hall are also particular. From the inner to the outer sections are a narrow table, a square table, and wooden chairs at its sides. A tea table and wooden chairs are placed at the sides of the hall. The sides of the square table stand the seats of the owner and his guests, on the further sides of which are for other guests. Notable are the furnishings on the narrow table, a large vase on the east end, and a standing mirror on the west end, and a pendulum clock in the middle. This layout means that males are on the left, and females are on the right, and that males do

business outside, safe and sound (homophonic with "vase"), and females are at home with a peaceful mind (homophonic with "mirror"). The strokes of the clock, the vase and the mirror imply "a peaceful mind of a lifetime (homophonic with 'strokes of the clock') for females, and safe and sound for males". The analogy of the clock to a lifetime began in the late Qing since the clock was not introduced into China until the late 19th century. On the sides of the clock are two hat stands. Some say that they are reserved for Chinese caps, and some say for paper rolls that light the smoking pipes, meaning that the fire of the family will never go out. The wing of the hall serves as the bedroom, and the wedding room for a son. The room is small, with a carved bed, a saddle table, domino stools, a closet, a fountain stool and other furniture. Though it looks somewhat crowded, the room radiates a warm feeling.

Woodcuts and color paintings, plaques, scrolls and scroll couplets, furniture and furnishings — these three elements constitute the unique style of interior decorations. Simplicity radiates a profound force, and reserve reflects cultural richness. Looking in every direction, one does not see the boredom of rigid beams, columns and boards, or a hodgepodge of valueless decorations. The simple woodcuts, calligraphy and paintings bring in blessings of luck and offer an esthetic sense of harmony.

Old houses, distant homes.

第二节 门窗木雕

徽州老房子的室内木雕，分布在门、窗、梁、柱、枋等构件上，以门窗上的木雕最多见。本节选择了3个古村的6幢名宅的部分门窗木雕，分别作以下介绍。

窗门
Window doors

窗栏板
Window board

窗栏板
Window board

窗栏板上的木雕
Woodcuts on window board

2.2　Woodcuts on doors and windows

The woodcuts are distributed on doors, windows, beams, columns and so on, mostly on the first two. This section introduces some of the door and window woodcuts from six old houses of three old villages.

大门上的大铜环
Knocker rings on the gate

眉板
Brow board

胸板
Chest board

腰板
Waist board

裙板
Skirt board

惜食非如惜財緣惜福

厢房莲花门
Lotus door to the wing

95

宏村"树人堂"汪氏九十一世祖汪星聚（1830—1888）建于1862年。木雕圆润朴拙，深浮雕精细，人物传神，题材丰富，寓意深刻。

Shurentang House, at Hongcun built in 1862 by Wang Xingju（1830-1888）, 91st ancestor of the Wang family. The carvings are of various themes and send profound messages. The woodcuts are smooth and simple, relief carvings elaborate, and figures lovely.

文王访贤。相传 2000 多年前，周文王到渭河边礼请谋士姜子牙入朝当丞相。
King of the Western Zhou visits sage. Legend has it that the king went to the Wei River to invite Jiang Ziya to be his prime minister.

孝感天地，二十四孝故事之一。孝子舜，感动了天地，大象为他耕田，尧帝将王位让给了舜。
Filial piety moves Heaven and Earth, one of the 24 stories of filial piety. Shun, symbol of filial piety, moved Heaven and earth, so that elephants helped him to cultivate farming land, and King Yao offered the throne to him.

用八仙的法器代表八仙的名号，暗八仙。汉钟离的扇子，铁拐李的葫芦。
The magic instruments used by the eight immortals indicate their Daoist names. Fan of Han Zhongli, and gourd of Tieguai Li.

韩湘子的笛子，张果老的鱼鼓。
Flute of Han Xiangzi, and fish drum of Zhang Guolao.

吕洞宾的宝剑，蓝采和的花篮。
Sword of Lü Dongbin, and flower basket of Lan Caihe.

曹国舅的玉版，何仙姑的荷花。
Jade board of Cao Guojiu, and lotus of He Xiangu.

蝙蝠象征福，桃子象征寿，铜钱象征禄，福禄寿三星高照。
The bat symbolizes happiness, the peach longevity, and the coin wealth.

宏村承德堂，建于清康熙末年（1720年）。清朝早期的木雕风格，线条流畅粗犷，大写意的画风，用河蚌壳粉末，土漆装饰木雕，色彩斑斓，画面更具魅力。

The Chengdetang House, at Hongcun, built in 1720 in the reign of Emperor Kangxi of the Qing. The woodcuts of the early Qing emphasized both smooth and rough lines, a general painting style. The carvings are decorated with shell powder and earth paint, creating a colorful charm.

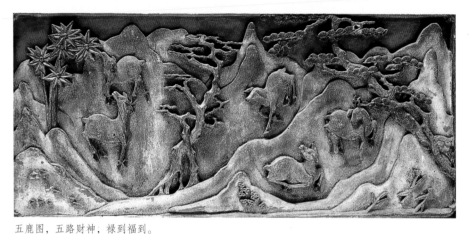

五鹿图，五路财神，禄到福到。
A picture of five deer symbolizes the coming of the five gods of wealth who deliver wealth and happiness.

五鹿图，子鹿吮乳，双鹿调情，温馨吉祥。
A picture of five deer. The infant deer suckle, and the adult deer flirt with each other, creating a familial feeling of warmth and good luck.

翠岭夜泊
Anchoring at the night of green hills

九曲回廊
A zigzag corridor

百舸争流
A hundred boats compete ahead

西溪塔影
Tower reflection in the Xixi river

小桥流水人家
Bridge, water, household

临水人家
Household at water side

西楼听水
Listening to water at Xilou

秋山月色
Moon at autumn hill

牧归
Return of the herd boy

冰清玉洁的乡村
Village in clear moonlight

宏村"承志堂",汪氏九十二世祖汪定贵建于清末。汪定贵（1842—1932），字廷魁。早年在上海、南京一带经销海产品，后来在九江市开糖业公司，任九江市商会副会长，生意兴隆，清末宏村的首富。
The Chengzhitang House, at Hongcun, built in the late Qing by Wang Dinggui, 92nd ancestor of the Wang family. Wang（1842–1932）, alias Tingkui, sold sea products in his early years in Shanghai and Nanjing, and later, opened a candy company in Jiujiang, and served as Vice–Chairman of Jiujiang Society of Commerce. With his enormous success, he became the richest merchant of Hongcun of the late Qing.
承志堂的木雕量多而精美，尤其是梁枋上的大幅木雕（见书后拉页）最为出色，人物众多，栩栩如生，生活气息浓郁，喜庆吉祥和欢乐。徽州木雕经过几百年的传承和创新，技法越来越纯熟，承志堂的木雕就是清末优秀木雕的代表作。
道家八仙的故事起始于宋元间的民间传说和戏本，成型于明嘉靖年间吴元泰著《八仙出处东游记》，"汉钟离、吕洞宾、张果老、铁拐李、曹国舅、蓝采和、韩湘子、何仙姑"八仙的形象和法器，在清朝中后期日趋固定，八仙的群体形象，非常适合渲染家居环境的快乐热闹、喜庆吉祥的喜庆气氛。
The woodcuts of the Chengzhitang House are abundant and elaborate, notably the large carvings on the beams（see gatefold at the end of the book）. Figures are numerous and lively, and carvings are full of life, happiness and luck. After hundreds of years, the woodcuts of Huizhou mature, and the woodcuts of the Chengzhitang House are a classic example.
The story of the eight Daoist immortals began with folk tales and opera scripts of the Song and Yuan dynasties, and took shape with *The Eight Immortals Journey East*, written by Wu Yuantai living in the Jiajing reign of the Ming. The images and instruments of the eight immortals, Han Zhongli, L ü Dongbin, Zhang Guolao, Tieguai Li, Cao Guojiu, Lan Caihe, Han Xiangzi, and He Xiangu, matured in the mid– and late Qing. The collective image of the eight immortals is particularly suitable for the atmosphere of happiness and luck in the household environment.

汉钟离，全真道教创始人，执芭蕉扇，代表"贵"。
Han Zhongli, founder of Real Daoism, carries a palm-leaf fan, symbolizing"nobility".

曹国舅，富家子弟，手执玉版，代表"富"。
Cao Guojiu, born of a rich family, carries a jade board, symbolizing"wealth".

铁拐李，借李瘸子之尸还魂成仙，拄拐杖，执葫芦，代表"病"。
Tieguai Li, becoming an immortal using the body of Cripple Li and walking with an iron stick, carries a gourd, symbolizing"disease".

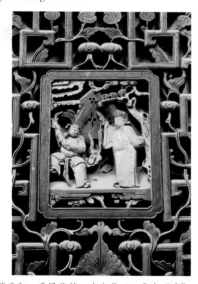

蓝采和，手提花篮，出身伶工，代表"贱"。
Lan Caihe, carries a flower basket, and works as an opera singer, symbolizing"humility".

吕洞宾，全真道教五祖之一，常度人成仙，背剑，代表"男"。
Lü Dongbin, one of the five ancestors of Real Daoism, and often using magic to turn mortals into immortals, carries a sword over his shoulders, symbolizing "male".

何仙姑，手执荷花，代表"女"。
He Xiangu, carries a lotus flower, symbolizing "female".

张果老，倒骑毛驴，执渔鼓，代表"老"。
Zhang Guolao, rides the donkey backwards and carries a fish drum, symbolizing "old age".

韩湘子，执笛子，代表"少"。
Han Xiangzi carries a flute, symbolizing "young age".

"福禄寿喜"是几千年中国传统社会向往的四种人生际遇。儿孙满堂、家业兴旺、家庭和睦、美满如意，乃有福之人；入仕升官，年有俸禄，乃富贵之人；心胸宽广，修身养性，天性乐观，延年益寿，乃高寿之人；大小喜事常常有，人逢喜事精神爽，乃随喜之人。

For thousands of years, "happiness, wealth, longevity and happy events" are the four occasions of one's life in the traditional society. One is said to be happy when he has a large, prosperous, close family; one is said to be wealthy when he is an official and has a steady annual income; one is said to have longevity when he is optimistic and lives a long life; and one is said to be full of happy events when he often has happy events and is in high spirits.

福
Happiness

禄
Wealth

寿
Longevity

喜
Happy events

雕刻有三国战事的元宝梁（宏村承志堂）
Bend beam carved with stories of the Three Kingdoms（Chengzhitang House, Hongcun）

雕刻祥云、兰草的元宝梁（关麓村）
Bend beam carved with clouds and orchids（Guanlucun）

桃花源里好耕田
Enjoying plowing in fairyland

火红的日子
Good days

宏村"桃园居"建于十九世纪六十年代。室内的木雕以清水雕见长，刻工十分细腻，画面简洁，题材丰富，给人清新脱俗的美感。

Taoyuanju House, at Hongcun, built in the 1860s. The house is noted for its pure water carvings of fine craftsmanship. With their simplicity and varied themes, they send a fresh and refined feeling.

上部：麒麟送子，喜鹊报喜。
Above: The kylin delivers a son and the magpie delivers good news.
下部：梅花寿桃，宝瓶宝鼎，福寿双全。
Below: Plums and longevity peaches, treasure vase and vessel symbolize happiness and longevity.

上图：麒麟送子，喜鹊报喜。
Above: The kylin delivers a son and the magpie delivers good news.
下图：松树盆景，瓶插桂花，宝瓶宝鼎，富贵长寿。
Below: Pine pot, and laurel in a treasure vase, symbolize wealth, nobility and longevity.

方天戟，寓意级级高升。福寿宝鼎，多福多寿。
Square halberd symbolizes promotion. Treasure vessel symbolizes happiness and longevity.

同心结与宝鼎，永结同心。
Love knot and treasure vessels symbolize eternal love.

万事如意图
Everything is as one wishes

钱鼎、寿鼎、福板，福禄寿。
Coin tripod, longevity tripod and happiness board symbolize wealth, happiness and longevity.

羲之爱鹅。东晋王羲之，大书法家。相传他从家鹅行水的姿态，悟出书法运笔之道，遂有爱鹅的癖好。

Geese, Wang Xizhi's favorite. Wang, living in the Eastern Jin, was a noted calligrapher. Legend has it that he realized the way of calligraphy from the postures in which geese swam, hence his predilection for geese.

和靖爱梅。宋代林逋，卒谥和靖先生，宅四周广种梅花，终日赏梅养鹤，不仕不婚，世称"梅妻鹤子"。

Plums, Mr. Hejing's favorite. Lin Bu, living in the Song, named posthumously Mr. Hejing, loved growing plums at home, fed cranes and never married. Hence the legend that "the plum was his wife and the crane was his son".

渊明爱菊。晋陶渊明喜养菊花。重阳节，太守王弘遣白衣人送酒到，陶公对菊醉酩。

Chrysanthemums, Tao Yuanming's favorite. Tao, living in the Jin, loved growing chrysanthemums. On Chongyang Festival, Wang Hong sent him wine, and Tao drank to his chrysanthemums until he is drunk.

茂叔爱莲。北宋周敦颐，字茂叔，著《爱莲说》"予独爱莲之出淤泥而不染"，遂有"茂叔爱莲"之说。

Lotus, Maoshu's favorite. Zhou Dunyi, alias Maoshu, wrote "Love for lotus": "I love the lotus only because it comes unsoiled out of the dirty mud". Hence the saying "Maoshu loves lotus".

厢房的莲花门，眉板是牡丹花，胸板荷花纹，四爱图的门心，腰板以菊花为底纹，刻之八宝图，裙板是"忠孝信义"图，清水雕温润细腻，层次分明，题材也契合家庭生活。

Lotus door to a wing, with peonies on the brow board and lotuses on the chest board. A door panel of four treasures, chrysanthemums on the waist board, carved with eight treasures, and "loyalty, filial piety, righteousness and justice" on the skirt board. The pure water carving is warm and fine, with good layering and of familial themes.

五彩庄塘的人家
Colorful household

塔川村"积余堂",清代建筑。门窗上的木雕图案,以乡村教育为题材。窗户上雕刻私塾、社学、府学、书院的教育场面。门上的16幅木雕,一幅木雕配一首唐宋诗,以诗画教育后代,独辟蹊径。

The Jiyutang House, at Tachuancun, built in the Qing. The patterns on its doors and windows take the theme of rural education. The windows are carved with scenes at the private school, shrine school, prefecture school and public school. Each of the 16 woodcuts on the doors was attached with a poem of the Tang or Song. Education with painting and poetry served as a new way of education.

福到眼前
Happiness arrives

"积余堂"东西两侧16扇莲花门腰板上的木雕,是依照16首《千家诗》的诗意设计雕刻的,并用蝇头小楷题诗于侧,诗情画意浑然天成。以古诗教育儿孙,耳濡目染,陶冶情操,也是中国传统教育的特色。

The woodcuts on the waist board of the 16 lotus doors on the east and west sides of the Jiyutang House are made in accordance with the poetic meanings of 16 poems in the *Book of Poetry*, and written in small regular script, sending idyllic feelings. Education with poetry is a special feature of traditional Chinese education.

答钟弱翁。牧童(宋)草铺横野六七里,笛弄晚风三四声。归来饱饭黄昏后,不脱蓑衣卧月明。

Reply to Zhongruoweng by Mu Tong (Song).
"Grass spreads across the open field, six, seven miles;
A flute plays in the evening breeze, three, four tunes.
He returns home, eats his fill, and when the dusk has ended,
Without removing his straw coat he lies down in the bright moonlight."

春夜。苏轼（宋）春宵一刻值千金，花有清香月有阴。歌管楼台声细细，秋千院落夜沉沉。
Spring night by Su Shi (Song).
"Spring night—one hour worth a thousand gold coins,
Clear scent of flowers, shadowy moon;
Songs and flutes upstairs—threads of sound,
In the garden, a swing, where night is deep and still."

村居即事。翁卷（宋）绿遍山原白满川，子规声里雨如烟。乡村四月闲人少，才了蚕桑又插田。
Village days by Weng Juan (Song).
"Green comes to hills, water white in all streams,
Cuckoos sing in a haze of rain.
Few are not busy in rural April,
Now mulberry leaves, now rice seedlings."

漫兴。杜甫（唐）糁径杨花铺白毡，占溪荷叶叠青钱。笋根稚子无人见，沙上凫雏傍母眠。
Random composition by Du Fu (Tang).
"The path is paved with poplar blossom, a carpet of white grain,
Lotus leaves on the little stream are piled like green coins.
Among the roots of new bamboo, pheasants no man has seen,
On the sand nearby, a duckling sleeps beside its mother."

湖上。徐元杰（宋）花开红树乱莺啼，草长平湖白鹭飞。风物晴和人意好，夕阳萧鼓几船归。
On the Lake by Xu Yuanjie (Song).
"Orioles chatter madly in trees of red blossoms,
Egrets converge on a lake of tall grass;
Everyone loves a clear mild day,
Boats return at dusk on waves of flutes and drums."

初夏睡起。杨万里（宋）梅子留酸溅齿牙，芭蕉分绿上窗纱。日长睡起无情思，闲看儿童捉柳花。
Getting up in early summer by Yang Wanli (Song).
"Plums begin to grow sour to the teeth,
Palms turn their green against the windows;
I listlessly rise from my nap,
Idly watching children grasp at willow flowers."

秋夕。杜牧（唐）银烛秋光冷画屏，轻罗小扇扑流萤。天街夜色凉如水，卧看牵牛织女星。
Autumn night by Du Mu (Tang).
"Her candle-light is silvery on her chill bright screen,
Her little silk fan is for fireflies.
She lies watching her staircase cold in the moon,
And two stars parted by the River of Heaven."

◀村晚。雷震（宋）草满寒塘水满陂，山衔落日浸寒漪。牧童归去横牛背，短笛无腔信口吹。
Village nightfall by Lei Zhen (Song).
"Grass fills ponds and water runs down slopes,
The sun sets on cool waves;
The herd boy returns home on ox back,
Blowing the flute with free tunes."

偶成。程颢（宋）云淡风轻近午天，傍花随柳过前川。旁人不识予心乐，将谓偷闲学少年。
Occasional composition by Cheng Hao (Song).
"High clouds, light wind, most noonday,
Walking by flowers and willows;
Passersby did not know my happy heart,
Thinking I was a youngster who never grows."

滁州西涧。韦应物（唐）独怜幽草涧边生，上有黄鹂深树鸣。春潮带雨晚来急，野渡无人舟自横。
West Stream at Chuzhou by Wei Yingwu (Tang).
"These I love: hidden plants that grow by the river's edge;
Above, yellow warblers in the deep trees singing;
Spring tides robed in rain, swifter by evening;
The ferry landing deserted where a boat swings by itself."

绝句。僧志南（宋）古木阴中系短篷，杖藜扶我过桥东。沾衣欲湿杏花雨，吹面不寒杨柳风。
Jueju by Seng Zhinan (Song).
"I moored my skiff by an old tree,
A walking stick helps me over a bridge to east.
An apricot-blossom rain is drizzling my robe,
While a Spring-willow breeze is caressing my face."

清明。杜牧（唐）清明时节雨纷纷，路上行人欲断魂。借问酒家何处有，牧童遥指杏花村。
Pure Brightness Festival by Du Mu (Tang).
"The ceaseless drizzles drips all the dismal day,
So broken-hearted fares the traveler on the way.
When asked where could be found a tavern bower,
A cowboy points to yonder village of the apricot flower."

◄绝句。杜甫（唐）两个黄鹂鸣翠柳，一行白鹭上青天。窗含西岭千秋雪，门泊东吴万里船。
Jueju by Du Fu (Tang).
"Two golden orioles sing amid the willows green;
A row of white egrets flies into the blue sky.
From my window the snow-crowned western hills are seen;
Beyond the door the east-bound ships at anchor lie."

夏日田园杂兴。范成大（宋）昼出耘田夜绩麻，村庄儿女各当家。童孙未解供耕织，也傍桑阴学种瓜。
Pastoral song on summer day by Fan Chengda（Song）.
"Men plows the fields in the day and women weave at night,
They work hard to their respective hearts;
Children, not knowing what plowing and weaving are,
But still like to stand by mulberry trees and watch melons."

枫桥夜泊。张继（唐）月落乌啼霜满天，江枫渔火对愁眠。姑苏城外寒山寺，夜半钟声到客船。
Mooring at Night by Maple Bridge by Zhang Ji（Tang）.
"The raven calls, the moon descends the sky with frost all white,
Near the bank maple, by a dim lamp I lie awake in sorrow.
And outside Gusu city, from Bleak Hill Temple, flow,
Out to the mooring boat the distant chimes of midnight."

社学，乡绅主办的乡级学校，官府给予资助，12 岁的儿童才能入学。图中自左至右：入学、训诫、苦读。

Shrine school, school officially funded and managed by country gentlemen. Only children of 12 and above can enter. From left to right: Entry, sermon, study.

书院，全国高级讲学教育学校。清代府州县乡亦设书院，广招生员，官府资助。乡村书院是儿童启蒙学校。

Public school, officially funded national school of high education. Public schools are also opened at the prefecture and county levels, enrolling students from various sources. The village public school is where village children receive their first-stage education.

◄社日。张演（唐）鹅湖山下稻粱肥，豚栅鸡栖对掩扉。桑柘影斜春社散，家家扶得醉人归。

Shrine Festival by Zhang Yan (Tang).
"By Goose Lake Mountain, rice and millet grown fat;
Half the pigpens and chicken coops shut for the night.
Mulberry, paper mulberry shadows slanting, the autumn festival dispersed,
Family after family holding up, helping their drunken ones home."

私塾。有私人聘请老师到家中教育儿孙，也有教书先生在村里收学生办私塾，学生少则几名，多则一、二十名。图中自左而右：双生贵子，哺乳。私塾上课。

Private school. Tutors teach the children of a family at home, or at the private school, sometimes several, and sometimes a dozen or more. From left to right: Twins suckle. Class at private school.

府学。府级官办学校，定员童生40名，后有增广。

Prefecture school, official school at the prefecture level, enrolling 40 students, and later a few more.

古村春色
Spring at old village

卢村"志诚堂",卢氏三十三世祖卢邦燮（1801—1866）建于十九世纪上半叶,清道光年间。"志诚堂"是徽州著名的木雕楼,举目四望,上下左右,皆木雕。雕工精美,题材十分广泛,既有世俗生活场景,又有丰富的历史典故,众多的画面就像一本固定在门窗上的图画书,厅堂成了儿孙启蒙的课堂,家人长年生活其间,也是一种很养眼的福气,好美的一个家。

The Zhichengtang House at Lucun, built in the first half of the 19th century in the reign of Emperor Daoguang of the Qing by Lu Bangxie（1801—1866）. The house is noted in Huizhou for its woodcuts, evident in every direction. The craftsmanship is elaborate and the themes varied, with both daily living scenes and rich historical stories. The numerous pictures make an excellent pictorial book fixed to doors and windows, and the hall serves as the classroom of child education. When family members live here for long, it is a pleasure of happiness and beauty.

志诚堂的木雕
Woodcuts at the Zhichengtang House

犬子苦读
Studying hard

牧歌一曲把家还
Returning home with a madrigal

会友图
Meeting friends

131

居家过日子
A day of living

雨中送客
Seeing guest off in the rain

放风筝，踏青乐
Joy of flying a kite

唐朝以来，民间以登科为折桂，今日桥上手持桂花的小孩，可能是未来登科之人，好兆头。
Since the Tang, passing the imperial examination has taken the custom of plucking a laurel branch. Today, children carrying a laurel flower on the bridge may pass the examinations in the future. What a good omen.

书生骑马进京赶考，路边一只猴子，取谐音，马上封侯。
A student rides a horse to the capital and takes the imperial examinations, with a monkey on the roadside, homophonic with "earl on the horse".

春耕插秧农夫忙
Planting rice seedlings in spring

千山万水赶考去
Going a long way for imperial examinations

乡村街头交易小景
Business at village street

筑土墙，盖新房，一家人正忙。
A family busy with building a new house of earth wall.

学富五车。清朝李汝珍著《镜花缘》第十六回："大贤世居大邦，见多识广，而且荣列校庠，自然才贯二酉，学富五车了"。五车书，形容读过很多书的人，学识渊博。

Great learning in five carts. Chapter 16 of *Flowers in the Mirror*, by Li Ruzhen of the Qing: "Five carts of books" refer to those who have great learning.

买臣负薪。朱买臣，汉朝人，家贫好学，卖柴度日，常担柴边行边诵书，五十岁才官升会稽太守。

Maichen carries firewood. Zhu Maichen, living in the Han, had a poor family but he loved reading. He had to sell firewood and often read while carrying his firewood on the way. He served as the prefect of Huiji Prefecture when he was 50 years old.

车胤囊萤。车胤，晋朝人，自幼好学，家贫夜读无灯，用白丝袋盛萤火虫，借光夜读，后来官居吏部尚书。

Che Yin reads by a bag of fireflies. Che Yin, living in the Jin, loved books, and because he had no lamp, used a bag of fireflies and read by the light of the fireflies. He later served as Minister of Official Personnel Affairs.

浪漫的"碧筒饮"。公元五世纪，魏晋时期，一位姓郑的官员，在济南大明湖游玩，割下湖中带茎子的荷叶，刺穿叶心通茎内，往荷叶里倒酒，人从荷茎的末端吸酒，清香爽口，妙不可言，人称"碧筒饮"。如此浪漫的饮酒方式，后来盛行于唐宋，流传于民间。画中老者正痴迷于"碧筒饮"，好快活的神仙日子。

The romantic "stem as straw drinking". In the 5th century, an official named Zheng, living in the Jin, took a trip to Daminghu Lake in Jinan. He cut off a lotus leaf, and pierced the leaf through the stem. He poured wine into the leaf, and sucked wine from the end of the stem as a straw. The drink was incredibly fresh and fragrant. Termed as "stem as straw drinking", this romantic drinking style popularized in the Tang and Song dynasties. The old man in the drawing enjoys himself like an immortal in stem as straw drinking.

驮起犁，赶着牛，春暖花开耕田忙。
Carrying a plow and driving a buffalo when spring warmth arrives and flowers bloom.

（上左图）苏武牧羊。苏武，汉朝中郎将，出使匈奴被扣留，派卫律说降，苏武坚贞不屈，住阴山大窟中，吃雪解渴，吃牛皮毡充饥，仗义牧羊，19年后始归。

Su Wu herds the sheep. Su Wu, general of the Han, was detained by the Xiongnu tribe. WeiLü was requested to ask him to surrender, but Su refused. He lived in a cave, and ate snow to quest his thirst and cowhide to quest his hunger. He herded sheep and did not return to the Han until 19 years later.

（上右图）伯乐相马。伯乐，春秋秦国人，善于相马。比喻善于发现人才的有识之士。

Bole judges horses. Bole, living in the Qin State of the Spring and Autumn Period, knew how to judge a good horse. The name is later used to refer to one who knows how to find talents.

（右图）孟浩然踏雪寻梅。孟浩然，唐代诗人，喜爱山水，尤爱梅花，曾经冒着大雪骑驴到灞陵去赏梅。

Meng Haoran seeks plums in snow. Meng Haoran, poet of the Tang, loved landscape, particularly plums. He once went to Baling to enjoy plums by riding a donkey through heavy snow.

诗书传家
The hand-down of poetry

撑船打鱼好开心
Fishing happily on the boat

香山九老，指的是唐代文人白居易、胡杲、吉玫、刘贞、郑据、卢贞、张浑、李元爽、神僧如满九位老者，他们因志趣相投，在洛阳香山结为"九老会"。香山与龙门石窟隔伊水相望，山清水秀，诗人白居易晚年隐居于香山寺，寄情山水，坐禅听经，自号"香山居士"，香山因九老而闻名。

The Nine of Xiangshan. The Nine of Xiangshan refers to the nine elder poets of the Tang, i.e., Bai Juyi, Hu Gao, Ji Mei, Liu Zhen, Zheng Ju, Lu Zhen, Zhang Hun, Li Yuanshuang, and Monk Ruman. They shared their interests, and formed the Nine Elders Society at Xiangshan of Luoyang. Xiangshan, separated from Longmen Grottoes by water, enjoys beautiful landscape. In his late years, Bai Juyi took hermitage at Xiangshan Temple. He showed passions for the landscape, would listen to the reading of the scriptures, and later termed himself as the Retired Scholar of Xiangshan.

竹林七贤。指的是晋朝的嵇康、阮籍、山涛、刘伶、阮咸、向秀、王戎七位文人志士，七人常聚会于竹林之中，尽情饮酒，各有主见和学问，并有鲜明的个性，后人称之"竹林七贤"。

Seven Sages of the Bamboo Grove. The Seven Sages of the Bamboo Grove refer to the seven men of letters, Ji Kang, Ruan Ji, Shan Tao, Liu Ling, Ruan Xian, Xiang Xiu and Wang Rong. They often gathered in a bamboo grove, drank to the best of their delight, and ventured their views and learning. They were later called the "Seven Sages of the Bamboo Grove".

第三节 挂络·斜撑·天花彩绘

徽州老房子的厅堂两侧过厢、回廊，在柱子之间常用挂络装饰，图案以花草、回字纹、祥云之类为多。斜撑、雀替、梁托、月枋、斗拱等都是梁柱之间的装饰构件，雕刻精美。厅堂、厢房的天花彩绘和戏台、祠堂的藻井彩绘，徽州也常见。

挂络与花窗
Hangings and decorated window

2.3　Hangings, slant supports and ceiling color paintings

The wings and corridors on both sides of the hall are often decorated with hangings, which usually follow the patterns of flowers and plants, character *hui*, and clouds. Slant supports, sparrow braces, beam hangers, crescent beams and bucket arches are all decorative fixtures between beams and columns, with elaborate carvings. Color paintings on the ceilings of halls and wings, and color paintings on the caissons of halls and wings at opera stages and ancestral houses are also common in the old houses of Huizhou.

古戏台前檐的装饰
Decorations on the front eaves of the old opera stage

天花板
Ceiling

双凤朝阳（天花彩绘）
Double phoenixes face the sun（ceiling color painting）

雕花悬柱
Carved suspended column

额枋、斜撑、雀替
Horizontal tablet, sparrow brace, slant support

雄狮戏球（斜撑）
Lion plays with the ball（slant support）

双狮戏球大券拱
Large arch of the two-lions-play-with-the-ball pattern

佛冠式藻井彩绘（古戏台）
Paintings on caissons（old opera stage）

传家有道惟存厚

三维挂络
3D hangings

第四节 堂匾·题额·楹联

堂名是厅堂的名称，也是房子的名称，寓意深刻。楷体大字，端庄大方。题额是边门、耳门、拱门的门楣上的题字，以示风雅。徽州人家厅堂上有挂楹联的习惯，既文气，又可以教育儿孙。

积余堂（塔川 堂匾）
Jiyutang House（Tachuan）

敦厚堂（宏村）
Dunhoutang House（Hongcun）

乐贤堂（宏村）
Lexiantang House（Hongcun）

敬义堂（李鸿章手书）
Jingyitang House（inscription written by Prime Minister Li Hongzhang）

松风（题额）
Song Feng（inscription）

邻溪书屋
Lingxi Public School

吾爱吾庐
I love my house

作退一步想
A step backward

2.4　Plaques, scrolls and scroll couplets

　　The hall name, both the name of a hall and the name of a house, sends profound messages. The name is written in regular script, and is noble. The scrolls are inscriptions on the top of side doors, ear doors and arch doors, and show elegance. Scroll couplets are usually hung on the walls of the hall. These couplets not only give a literary sense but also are instructive.

百可园
Baikeyuan Garden

东园 East Garden

西递 Xidi

百年老中堂老对联仍然挂在厅堂上，显得古朴雅致。
The century-old scroll couplets still hang on the wall of the hall, dainty and elegant.

西园 West Garden

留月 Liu Yue（inscription）

一庭之中有至乐　六经以外无奇书
Ultimate pleasure in one courtyard Boring books except six classics

二字箴言惟勤惟俭　两条正路曰读曰耕
Two-word saying: Diligence and frugality Two-paths: reading and plowing

皓月当空若镜临水　春雨润木自叶流根
High moon in the sky is reflected as a mirror in water Spring rain moistens trees from leaf to roots

美景良辰赏心乐事　英词妙墨好古多闻
Great sights great moments great pleasure Excellent poems excellent paintings excellent knowledge

便宜多自吃亏来　快乐每从辛苦得
Convenience comes from losses Pleasure comes from hardships

蔬粥余风宜承先志　诗书世业重冀后人
Porridge inherits the ways of ancestors Poetry places hope on descendents

松性淡逾古　鹤情高不群
Pines aim low to live a long life Cranes are ambitious to make a lonely living

真味书田菽粟　异香心地芝兰
Real taste like beans Sweet heart like orchids

孝弟传家根本　诗书经世文章
Piety makes prosperous families Poetry makes good readings

几百年人家无非积善　第一等好事只是读书
Century-old families do only good deeds Top-one priority is just hard reading

第五节　摆设与家具

徽州人家的厅堂正中，摆放长条几、八仙桌、太师椅，长条几上中间摆放自鸣钟，东边摆瓷瓶，西边摆座镜，钟两边摆瓷器帽筒，家具摆放，对称雅致。房间内有雕花木床、马鞍桌、凳、衣橱等，既实用又美观。

2.5　Furnishings and furniture

In the middle of a hall stand a long narrow table, a square table and wicket armchairs. In the middle of the narrow table is placed a pendulum clock, with a vase on the east end of the table and a standing mirror on the west end. On the immediate sides of the clock are placed porcelain and a hat stand. This layout gives a symmetric sense. A carved wood bed, a saddle table, some stools and a closet in the bedroom are both practical and pretty.

后厅住的是老人，长条几中间摆放福禄寿三星瓷像（宏村承志堂）。
The elders live in the back hall. In the middle of the long narrow table are placed porcelain images of happiness, wealth and longevity. (Chengzhitang House, Hongcun)

徽州人家厅堂上的流行摆设，长条几，八仙桌椅、茶几，长条几上东边大瓷瓶，西边座镜，中间一座自鸣钟，钟的两侧是一对瓷帽筒。

The common furnishings include a long narrow table, a square table and wicket armchairs. In the middle of the narrow table is placed a pendulum clock, with a vase on the east end of the table and a standing mirror on the west end. On the immediate sides of the clock are placed two porcelain hat stands.

承志堂下厅仪门、鱼缸
Door and fish bowl in the lower hall of the Chengzhitang House

精雕细刻，金碧辉煌，富贵和温馨都停留在这里（木雕楼的雕花床）
Finely carved and magnificent like gold. Wealth, nobility and warmth never leave here (Carved bed at woodcut house)

志诚堂的摆设
Furnishings at the Zhichengtang House

第三章
古村的历史公共建筑
Chapter Three
Public architecture of old villages

月沼的早晨
Morning at the Crescent Pool

冬日里的慵懒也是一种福分（宏村南湖）
Laziness in winter is a pleasure (South Lake, Hongcun)

第一节 引言

徽州的乡村社会里，每个人的亲族交往都有一个生活圈子，父母妻子儿女，是血缘关系最亲的人，当然也是最贴近自己的家庭小圈子，兄弟姐妹、伯叔姑舅姨、堂兄弟姐妹、表兄弟姐妹……由近亲到远亲，一圈套一圈地向社会发散开去。在这个亲族圈子里，有一个十分明确的区别：门内人和门外人。门，不是房子的门，而是以男性传承为主线的宗族之门。女人嫁到丈夫家，就是夫家的门内人，自然会事事为夫家着想，娘家人就是门外人。男性家族一代一代繁衍下去，兄弟、堂兄弟、族兄弟……村子里同一姓氏的族系会越来越复杂，于是，族人会从某一代开始分

房头认祖宗，立字辈，为了祭祀共同的祖先，团结族人求得社会生存的空间，族人会倾其所有集资建造宗族祠堂。今天保存下来的数百幢祠堂，数量上已经是当年的很小一部分，但是，其中仍然不乏久负盛名的大祠堂，从中不难想象当年的族人耗费了多少财力、物力、人力和精力，才能建成如此美轮美奂的杰出建筑，可见当年徽商财力之雄厚，宗族观念之强烈，绝非一般。

祠堂，首先是族人祭祀祖先、编修家谱的地方。祭祀祖先，可以唤起族人对祖先的记忆，对同族人血缘关系的认同感。高大、宽敞、威严、肃穆的祠堂里，摆放着祖先容像、牌位、供品，燃

154

起香烛，青衣奏乐，族长领班，全体叩拜，严肃追思的气氛，对每个族人的心灵都是一次历史的洗礼。

祠堂，是族人举行婚丧仪式的场所。族人娶媳妇，新娘子都是在祠堂里下轿子，象征着新娘子已经是家族的门内人。族人家里生了男孩子，祠堂里有专人登记在册。家族里病逝在家中的成年人，都在祠堂里举行治丧仪式，逝者的牌位也留在祠堂后厅的享堂里，供族人祭祀。家家在祠堂里举行婚丧仪式，给每个人的生命、每个家庭的延续都打上了深深的宗族烙印。

祠堂，是宗族延续的建筑场所；家谱，就是宗族延续的文字载体。各个姓氏家族数十年要编修一次家谱，从资金筹集，逐户人丁登记，编辑，雕版，印刷，祭谱，毁版等一系列工序，都是在祠堂里完成的。每一个家庭的延续汇集一处，成了整个宗族的延续，每一个人的根都在谱里，宗谱也是整个宗族的根。

祠堂也是族人议事的地方。族里的田产店铺的管理，村里公共设施的投资，与外村外姓人的纠纷处置，族里的重大节庆活动的组织筹备，族人违犯了族规的处罚，都是族长与长辈们议决的事项。当年，乡村是以宗族管理的方式实现村庄自治，保持社会稳定。由于国家财力的限制，国家行政管理仅仅延伸到县级，乡村地方行政管理是依靠宗法制度实现的，所以，村庄的宗族管理是得到政府

万松林间泉水清（南屏）
Clear spring in the pine grove
(Nanping)

大力支持的。但是，族长的专制式统治，也必然伤害了族人的尊严，尤其是对有失贞节的妇女的残酷惩处，更是令人发指。

留存到今天的大大小小的祠堂，建筑恢宏，装饰精美，身临其境，惊叹之余，似乎看到了千百年间族人哭于斯，乐于斯，大家族大团聚的场面，似乎看到了族人中举的进士匾，皇上赐封的功德匾在祠堂里挂得重重叠叠，也似乎看到了受责的妇女的行行泪滴滴血。看得见的祠堂建筑，留在今天，看不见的喜怒哀乐，留在了昨天。

历史上的中国乡村，从家庭到国家，妻子服从丈夫，儿子服从父亲，臣子服从君王，一直是全社会奉行的准则。为了让准则深入人心，一方面严惩违反准则的人，另一方面大力表彰"先进典型"，为忠臣、孝子、义士、贞女、烈妇树牌坊，就是表彰典型的特殊方式。牌坊是用巨石精雕细刻树立在街头、村头行人容易看到的地方，明清时代徽州的牌坊，无论是数量之多，还是建筑结构之复杂多变，雕刻之精美，在全国也是首屈一指的。今天徽州留存下来的几十座牌坊，就让世人惊咤不已。

村里树牌坊，要么是皇上降旨，要么是官方批准，对地方上都是一件非常荣耀的大事，好比今天立纪念碑一样。固然，我们不能用今天的人权意识去评判当年的忠臣孝子，但是，我们也不得不为当年的贞女烈妇喊一声冤，男人可以三妻四妾、宿花眠柳，为什么妇女只能终身守寡、为夫殉节？贞节牌坊是夫权社会强加给妇女的精神枷锁。不做婊子，不要牌坊，还我尊严与自由！这是文明社会废弃牌坊的心灵呐喊！只是，要摧毁的应该是精神上的牌坊，街头田间的精美牌坊，是应该珍惜保护的文化遗产，留给后人的是心灵的震撼。

徽州的商人，不但有精明的商业头脑，而且富有远见的文明意识。商业上的巨大成功，使他们更清楚自己的社会地位的脆弱，更清楚自己的店铺应该传给更具文化素质的子弟才能长盛不衰，更清楚家族后代应该如何去适应城市文明生活的潮流，希望都在教育上。徽商非常重视子弟的教育，一方面在家乡倾力投资办学，建书院办私塾，一方面尽力资助子弟就读。家族中若有子弟能够读书中举，步入仕途，当然是家族的荣耀，也是徽商竭力争取的官方依靠。大部分的子弟还是接受了启蒙教育以后，打下了一定的文化基础，为日后的经商生涯和社会生活做好素质准备。徽州有一副楹联："读书好营商好效好便好，创业难守成难知难不难"。无论读书经商，只要成效好，便都是成功的人生。徽商是多么讲究实际！徽州的乡村书院是学童的启蒙书院，留下的已经不多，现存较完整的乡村书院有宏村的南湖书院、歙县雄村的竹山书院，前者建在南湖之畔，后者坐落在新安江之滨，湖光山色，环境幽美，真是学童启蒙的好地方。

古村的街道、店铺、古桥、亭阁和供水系统，都是古村方便村民生活的公共建筑。古村的店铺作坊是村民生活必需品的供应商，前店后坊，前店后家的店铺很多，小本生意多，店铺的结构和门面装饰都很简陋。但是，家乡小店与八方乡亲都很亲热很熟悉，大家都喜欢到店里去聊聊，顺带买点东西，小店的生意也算可以。半个世纪以来，随着现代商业的巨大冲击，老街老店已经罕见。休宁县万安镇百年老街，数百米长的老街，上门板的老店铺，弯弯的石板

开心过日子（木俑）
Spending happy days（Wooden figures）

路，几乎还是百年前的老样子，少数店铺还在营业，多数老房子还住人，一条百年老街还保存得如此真实如此完整，真是徽州的孤例，非常珍贵。

徽州古村依山傍水，水资源都是比较丰富的。但是，取水用水的便利，古村的水景风光，各个村又是有差别的。建设一座古村，先人能够先挖水渠引水进村，然后建房兴村，为村民生活提供洁净、方便、丰富的山溪水，为全村创造一个动静结合的美丽的水景环境，延绵六百年到今天，能有如此巧妙的人工古水系的古村，全徽州也只有宏村。宏村的月沼、南湖，举世闻名，宏村的人工古水系，是成功的村庄供水系统和杰出的公共建筑。

徽州古村的历史公共建筑，是时代的产物。街道、供水系统等是村民生活的基础设施，祠堂是村庄自治管理和社会活动的中心，书院、戏台和神庙是村民教育与文化生活的场所，牌坊就是村庄道德形象的标志。这些公共建筑不同的功能，构建了千百年的徽州乡村的社会生活，它们既反映了当年的生产力水平，又反映了当年徽州乡村社会生活的管理方式和价值观。

今天，我们既为这些留存下来的精美建筑作品的工艺水平、施工技术和工程难度而惊叹，也为人杰地灵的徽州人民创造自己的美丽家园和幸福生活的智慧勇气和艰苦劳动而倍感自豪，也为千百年间古村里发生的礼教吃人的斑斑血泪而震惊，更为今天的徽州人民能够更理性地保护、研究、利用精美的徽州建筑和辉煌的徽州文化，创造出更富裕更民主更和谐的新徽州新文明而充满希望，看得见希望的日子，就在眼前。

森林里的老屋
Old house in the grove

3.1 Introduction

In the village society of Huizhou, every one has his own circle of relationship. Parents, wives and children are the closest blood ties, and of course constitute the closest familial circles. The family is then extended to brothers and sisters, uncles and aunts, male and female cousins on the paternal side, and male and female cousins on the maternal side. In the core and extended circles, there exists a clear distinction: those behind the door, and those outside the door. Of course, this door does not refer to the door to a house, but the line of clanship centered on male descendents. When females are married, they become "those behind the door" at the homes of their husbands, and they must think for everything at their husbands' homes. Members that were close to them now become "those outside the door". On the male side, a family extends down generations, i.e., brothers, cousins and distant cousins, and thus the clan relations grow increasingly complex. In the end, clan members begin to designate their ancestors, and to memorize the ancestors and to seek better space for social welfare, and members of the same clan spend every coin to build the ancestral house. The hundreds of ancestral houses preserved from former times are only a portion of the number of ancestral houses in the old days, but the many renowned ancestral houses still remind

us of how much wealth and energy a clan spent in constructing those perfect works of architecture. One can also imagine the richness of Huizhou merchants of the old days and their sense of clan identity.

Ancestral houses are where members of the clan pay respects to ancestors and compile family trees. Paying respects to ancestors brings back memories for the ancestors and an identity of blood ties of the clan. In the spacious and serene house are placed the portraits, tablets and sacrifices of the ancestors of a clan. When the incense is burned, and ceremonial music is played, the head of the clan leads all clan members to bow and worship. Each occasion is a baptism of the mind of each member.

Ancestral houses are also where weddings and funerals are held. When a member gets married, the bride must get out of her sedan at the ancestral house, a symbol that the bride now becomes a member of "those behind the door". When a boy is born, the birth must be registered. When an adult member dies, a funeral ceremony is held for him at the ancestral house, and his tablet will be placed in the memorial room of the back hall of the house. Each family holds these ceremonies here, which offers a deep impression of clanship on each life.

Ancestral houses are the sites of clan extension; family trees are the carriers of that extension. Each dozens of years, the family tree is revised. The whole process, from fundraising, door-to-door registration, editing, printing, family tree worship to the destruction of the old block, is completed at the ancestral house. The extension of each family, when collected, becomes part of the extension of the entire clan. The roots of each individual enter the family tree, and the clan family tree becomes the roots of the entire clan.

Ancestral houses are also reserved for clan discussions. The management of fields and stores, the investment of public facilities in the village, the disposal of conflicts with members of another village or another surname in the village, the organization of important celebrations, and the solutions to clan violations, are items of discussions among the head and senior members of the clan. Formerly, a village was self-governed for social stability in the form of clan management. Due to limited state resources, the state government stopped at the county level, and so the management at the village level had to depend on the clan system. As a result, clan management was encouraged by the government. Of course, the dictatorial government of any clan head would inevitably bring injury to members of the clan, in particular the cruel punishment of females that lost their moral integrity.

The ancestral houses of varying sizes that are preserved to today are magnificent and finely decorated. When one is at the house, one can easily imagine the cries, the joys, and the gatherings of clan members in the past centuries. Here also, one seems to see the tablet inscriptions of the imperial scholars who pass the imperial examinations, the many virtue tablets conferred by the emperor, and the tears and blood of women that are punished therein. The visible house is preserved to today; the invisible joy and sorrow is left to yesterday.

The Chinese villages in history observed the principle, from family to state, that wives must obey their husbands, sons their fathers, and ministers their lords. For this principle to take roots in every mind, violations were severely punished, and "good models" were praised. One typical method of praise was to establish memorial archways for loyal ministers, pious sons, righteous gentlemen, women of integrity, and vengeful women. Memorial archways are established at obvious sites, such as streets or accessible points to passersby, with elaborately carved stones. The memorial archways of Huizhou in the Ming and Qing rank first across the nation, not only in their number, but also in their complexity of architecture and carving skill.

Establishing archways in the village, either in accordance with the emperor's edict or by other official approval, is a glory to the local area, an honor very much similar to establishing a monument in the present day. Of course, one cannot evaluate the ministers or sons by the principle of human rights of today, but one has to say a word of justice for the women of the former days. Why could men take three wives or four concubines, or seek pleasure in prostitution, while women must be widows who could never take new husbands? Women's integrity archways were the bondage imposed on women in a male-dominated society. "I shall never be a prostitute; I shall never want an archway; I shall only want dignity and liberty!"— this is a yell of the mind that archways must be abolished in a civilized society. Of course, what must be abolished are the spiritual archways; those around the fields and on the village streets are a cultural legacy that give the shock of the mind and must thus be protected.

Huizhou merchants had not only a head for business but a far-sighted cultural awareness. Their enormous business success led them to be aware that their social status was low, that their stores must be handed down to their children if these stores would ever grow, and that their descendents must know how to adapt themselves to the trends of urban civilization. All this depended on education. The merchants stressed education. To that end, on the one hand, they invested heavily in the establishment of public and private schools; on the other hand, they funded student expenses. Whenever anyone passed the imperial examinations or went to officialdom, they would deem this as familial glory and the official support that they themselves could depend on. The primary education laid some cultural basis for most students, which would prepare themselves for the coming business careers and social life. As a couplet of Huizhou goes, "Good schooling and good business comes down to good results; difficult career and difficult maintenance amounts to bewaring of difficulty". That is, whether in schooling or in business, good results mean the success of one's life. What a practical mind that Huizhou merchants had! The public schools were where school-age children received their first-stage education. Not many of these schools remain to today; two that are preserved intact are South Lake School of Hongcun, and Zhushan School of Xiongcun of Xixian County. The former stands by South Lake, and the latter is situated by the Xinanjiang River, with its blue water, green hills, and quiet environment.

The streets, stores, bridges, pavilions and water-supply system are the public architecture that provided convenience to villagers. The stores and workshops provided daily commodities, with the store in front and the workshops at the back, great in number. The stores had simple structures and crude decorations. However, these local stores were close to villagers from all directions, who went chatting and shopping in passing. As a result, the business of the store was handsome. For half a century, with the impact of modern commerce, one does not find many of these streets or stores now. Only a few of them remain what they were hundreds of years ago. The old street at Wanan of Xiuning is hundreds of meters long, with old stores that close their doors daily using door planks, and with a curvy

绩溪县龙川胡氏宗祠内"荷花系列"木雕精选
Selected woodcarvings series of "water lily" preserved in Hu's ancestral house in Longchuan of Jixi County

board road. Only a few such stores are still open, but most of the old houses are still in use. This street is the only example in which such old streets are preserved so well.

The old villages have green hills and surrounding water: water resources are rich here. However, villages differ from each other in the convenience of water supply, and in the water sights. To build a village, the ancestors had first to dig a ditch to lead water to the village, and must then build houses, in order to provide clean and rich stream water to village life, and to create a pleasant water sight environment that combined motion and quiet. After six centuries, Hongcun is the only one that has such an elaborate water system. The Crescent Pool and South Lake are now world-renowned, and the ancient water system is an enormous success of a village water supply system and work of public architecture.

The public architecture is a product of its age. The streets and water supply system constitute the infrastructure of the villagers and their life. The ancestral house is the center of autonomous administration and social activity. The schools, opera stages and temples are the sites where villagers engage in education and cultural activities. The memorial archways serve as the symbol of village ethics. These public structures, designed for different purposes, have created a social life of Huizhou villages for hundreds of centuries: they reflect both the productivity of their times, and the modes of management and standards of values of social life.

Today, we admire the ingenuity, techniques and difficulty in constructing these works of elaborate architecture. We find pride in the wisdom and labor that the people here spent on their beautiful homes and happy life. We are shocked at the blood shed because of feudal ethics that occurred in the old villages. We are also full of hope that Huizhouans of today are protecting, studying and utilizing the architecture and culture more rationally, and are creating a richer, more democratic and more harmonious culture. Days of new hope are right ahead.

第二节　祠堂与戏台

古徽州六个县留存下来的古祠堂尚有300多幢，保存完整、装饰精美的大祠堂，五百年前的明代祠堂，祠堂、戏台、观戏台三位一体的祠堂，不乏其例。大门楼、门厅、大天井、正厅、亨堂，三进五开间的结构，是徽州祠堂的普通规制，书里留下了它们的身影。

屏山古祠光裕堂（俗称"菩萨厅"）
The Guangyutang House, old ancestral house at Pingshan（popularly known as the Buddha Hall）

3.2　Ancestral houses and opera stages

More than 300 ancestral houses remain from former times in the six counties of old Huizhou. They include large ancestral houses that are well preserved and elaborately decorated, ancestral houses of the Ming, and ancestral houses combining the house, opera stage and audience stand. A large arch gate, a doorway hall, a large skylight, a hall, a memorial hall, this five-room structure was the usual structure for an ancestral house. The readers can find them in this book.

族长议事的地方（屏山）
Site of clan discussions（Pingshan）

庭院深深　满目沧桑（屏山庆余堂）
Deep courtyard after vicissitudes（Qingyutang House, Pingshan）

西递村胡氏总祠敬爱堂大门楼
Arch gate to the Jingaitang House, Hu's ancestral house, at Xidicun.

宏村汪氏宗祠"乐叙堂"大厅，汪氏 76 世祖汪思齐建于 1423 年。
The great hall named "Lexutang" of Wang's ancestral house in Hongcun was built by the 76th ancestor Wang Siqi in 1423.

祖宗容像
Portraits of ancestors

西递祠堂追慕堂大门楼
Arch gate to the Zhuimutang House, ancestral house at Xidicun

南屏村叶氏祠堂占地2000平方米，三进五开间，80根巨大屋柱，威严肃穆。
Ye's Ancestral House of Nanping covers an area of 2 000 sq m, of the five-room structure, with 80 thick columns. The house looks serene and magnificent.

绩溪县龙川胡氏宗祠大门楼。龙川是明朝嘉靖年间兵部尚书胡宗宪的家乡。
Gate house of Hu's ancestral hall in Longchuan of Jixi County.Longchuan was the defense minister Hu Zongxian's hometown in Ming dynasty emperor Jiajing period.

婺源县汪口俞氏宗祠内景
Yu's Ancestral House at Wangkou of Wuyuan County

俞氏宗祠大屋檐及木雕
Large eaves and woodcuts at Yu's Ancestral House

歙县呈坎村罗东舒先生祠——宝纶阁
Baolunge, Luo Dongshu's House at
Chengkancun of Xixian County

宝纶阁的雕花大屋顶
Carved roof of Baolunge

祁门县新安乡株林村古祠余庆堂的戏台（坐南朝北）。建于清同治年间（1862—1874 年）。上厅是祠堂，下厅是戏台，两侧是观戏楼，中间是天井庭院。戏台分后台和前台，两侧有对称的4个侧门，供演员上下台用，雕饰戏文、花鸟，绮丽华贵。祠堂正厅既是宗族活动场所，又是观戏时的观众座席，非常实用。

Opera stage of Yuqingtang House, at Zhulincun of Qimenxian County, built in the reign of Emperor Tongzhi of the Qing (1862 — 1874). The upper hall serves as the ancestral house. The lower hall serves as the opera stage, with the audience stand on both sides, and the skylight courtyard in the middle. The opera stage is divided into the front-and backstage, with four side doors, reserved for actors and actresses, and carved with opera words, or flowers and birds. The hall of the ancestral house is the center of clan activity and acts as the audience stand.

坑口村祠堂及两侧观
戏台（坐北朝南）
Ancestral house and
audience stands on the
sides at Kenkoucun
ancestral house（facing
south）

祁门县闪里坑口村祠堂里的古戏台，宽敞一些，结构和装饰也很精美。（坐南朝北）
Opera stage at Kenkoucun ancestral house, spacious and with elaborate structure and decorations.（facing
north）

余庆堂古戏台的前檐装饰
Decorations on the front eaves of the Yuqingtang House

拱顶
Arch roof

第三节 牌坊与亭阁

半个世纪前，徽州的大村子都有石牌坊，尽管现存的牌坊只有区区几十座，仍然可以看到中国乡村古代纪念碑的建筑艺术，也可以想象当年乡村的族人既要炫耀家族的荣誉于世人和后代，又把"忠孝节义"的道德伦理固化在石头上遗传千秋。只是，文明的潮流已经吞没了反人性的礼教，留下的是珍贵的建筑遗产和传统文化的历史佐证。

歙县唐模村同胞翰林牌坊，建于清康熙年间（1622—1722）为表彰康熙年间进士许承宣、许承家兄弟而建。

Brothers'memorial archway at Tangmocun of Xixian County, built in the reign of Emperor Kangxi of the Qing（1622—1722）in honor of the brothers Xu Chengxuan and Xu Chengjia, imperial scholars who passed the imperial examinations in the reign of Emperor Kangxi.

3.3 Memorial archways and pavilions

Half a century ago, each large village had stone archways. Though there are only dozens of them, the art of ancient monument architecture of Chinese villages remains evident, and one can still imagine that clan members of the villages of the former times wished to hand down the familial glory and solidify the ethics of "loyalty, filial piety, integrity and righteousness" on stone. It is only that the following trends of culture have already gulfed the anti-human etiquette, leaving behind the evidence of precious architectural heritage and traditional culture.

歙县城内许国牌坊。建于明万历十二年（1584），为表彰明代礼部尚书兼武英殿大学士许国平息云南叛乱有功而建。牌坊是非常罕见的八脚牌坊，结构雄伟，雕刻精美。
Xu Guo's memorial archway in the seat of Xixian County, built in 1584, 12th year of the Wanli reign of the Ming, in honor of Xu Guo, who conquered the Yunnan Rebellion. This archway is rare in that it has eight feet, with a magnificent structure and elaborate carvings.

歙县郑村的"贞白里坊",建于元代（1271 — 1368），徽州现存的最古老的牌坊，表彰郑千龄（贞白先生）一家三代乡贤而建。
Zhenbai's memorial archway, at Zhengcun of Xixian County, built in the Yuan（1271—1368）, the oldest archway in Huizhou, in honor of the three generations of the family of Zheng Qianling（"Mr. Zhenbai"）.

歙县丰口村四脚牌坊建于明嘉靖年间（1522 — 1566），为表彰乡贤郑廷宣、郑绮父子而建。
Four-foot memorial archway at Fengkoucun of Xixian County, built in the reign of Emperor Jiajing of the Ming（1522 — 1566）in honor of Zheng Tingxuan and his son Zheng Yi.

歙县雄村的"四世一品"坊。建于十九世纪七十年代，表彰清乾隆年间户部尚书曹文埴而建。曹文埴、曹振镛父子皆为清朝的一品官。
"First-rank Officials" memorial archway, at Xiongcun of Xixian County, built in the 1870s in honor of Cao Wenzhi, Minister of Revenues in the reign of Emperor Qianlong of the Qing. Cao and his son Cao Zhenyong were both first-rank officials.

棠越牌坊群
Torii group in Tangyue

歙县许村的廊桥"高阳桥"、"双寿承恩"牌坊（为一对百岁寿星夫妇而建）、大观亭，亭、坊、桥三者并列，立于村中，蔚为壮观。
Memorial archway at Xucun of Xixian County in honor of a centenarian couple. Daguan Pavilion, archway and bridge stand together in the village, a picture of magnificence.

许村大观亭，建于明嘉靖年间（1522—1566），三层砖木结构，第一、二层八角，第三层四角，飞檐翘角，极具地标意义的建筑物。

Daguan Pavilion at Xucun, built in the reign of Emperor Jiajing of the Ming（1522—1566）, with a three-story brick and wood structure, the first two stories being octagonal and the top story being quadrigonal, a label of the village.

许村五马坊，位于大观亭北侧。建于明正德二年（1507），为明代洪武年间（1368—1398）曾任汀州知府（雅称"五马"）的许伯升所立。

Wuma memorial archway, at Xucun, situated on the north of Daguan Pavilion, built in 1507, 2nd year of the Zhengde reign of the Ming, by Xu Bosheng, Prefect of Tingzhou Prefecture in the reign of Emperor Hongwu of the Ming（1368—1398）.

许村村口的薇省坊，建于明嘉靖年间，为湖广参政许珀所建。薇省，是中书省的旧称，朝庭的一个部门。薇省坊后面是"三朝典翰"坊，是为明朝中书舍人汪德章、汪伯爵而立。
Weisheng memorial archway at the entrance to Xucun, built in the Jiajing reign of the Ming by Xu Guan, Vice Commissioner of Four Provinces. Weisheng is the former name for Secretariat. Behind the archway is the Three−Court Drafter memorial archway, built in honor of Wang Dezhang and Wang Bojue, drafters of the Ming.

许村双节孝坊，清嘉庆年间建（1796 — 1820 ），高4.7米，宽2.9米，是徽州最小的一座牌坊，为表彰许俊业的继妻金氏和小妾贺氏两人节孝而立，也是用她们纳鞋底的微薄积蓄所建。
Memorial archway of double righteousness and filial piety, at Xucun, built in the Jiaqing reign of the Qing（1796 — 1820 ）, the smallest archway in Huizhou, which is only 4.7m high and 2.9m wide. The archway was built in honor of Jin, second wife of Xu Junye and He, his concubine, using their savings from making shoe soles.

第四节 书院与私塾

　　徽州古村里的书院，不同于州府县城里的书院。与今天的小学、中学的区别相近。古村里的书院，老师多了，学生多了，老师有了分工，比一位教书先生收几个学生的私塾进了一步。书院是古村近代文明的象征，孩子启蒙教育的殿堂。

宏村南湖书院，位于南湖北岸，建于清嘉庆十九年（1814），是宏村汪授甲、汪以文等人集资筹建，名曰："以文家塾"。
South Lake School, at Hongcun, located north of South Lake, was built in 1814, 19th year of the Jiaqing reign of the Qing, with the donations of Wang Shoujia and Wang Yiwen of Hongcun, hence "Yiwen Private School".

德行很高的人都留存着童真般的天性（圣人孩之，宏村碧园）
Childhood innocence always follows men of great virtue（Biyuan, Hongcun）

3.4 Public and private schools

The public schools in the old villages of Huizhou differ from the public schools in prefecture and county seats, a difference similar to that between primary and high schools of today. As the public schools grew, there were more students and more teachers, and teachers began to have division of labor. This practice was a step further than in private schools where a teacher took only a few students. The public school was a symbol of modern civilization in old villages, where children received their first-stage education in their lives.

南湖书院的讲堂
Lecture room at South Lake school

南湖书院的文昌阁，学童入学祭拜孔子的地方。
Wenchangge, at South Lake School, is where students pay respects to Confucius.

天真的童年，启蒙的日子（私塾）
Innocent childhood, enlightening days（Private school）

"学做好人"歙县许村小学墙上的题字（20世纪 20年代）
"Learn to Do Good Deeds", inscription on the wall of Xucun Primary School of Xixian County （1920s）

春到书院
Spring comes to school

歙县雄村"竹山书院",建于1755—1759年,曹翰屏所建,占地1130平方米。内有讲堂、清旷轩,轩前有庭院,当年族中规定"子弟中举者可在院中栽桂花树一棵",今尚存桂花树20余棵,后人称之"桂花厅",明清两代雄村出过进士30人,举人24人,文脉雄厚。院内建有一座文昌阁八角亭。

Zhushan School, at Xiongcun of Xixian County, built between 1755—1759, covers an area of 1 130 sq m. It has lecture rooms and the Qingkuang Studio, with a courtyard in front of it. In former times it was ruled that "those who pass the imperial examination can plant a laurel tree in the courtyard", and today, over 20 trees remain. It was called "Laurel Hall". In the Ming and Qing, Xiongcun produced 30 imperial scholars and 24 first-degree scholars. An octagonal pavilion, called Wenchangge, stands in the courtyard.

当年中举者一人栽一棵桂花树,今天蔚然一片,历史在这里积淀

Each successful test-taker planted a sweet-scented osmanthus tree, leaving behind a stretch of history

桂花厅里举人多
First-degree scholars abound in the Laurel Hall

文昌阁，两层八角木结构，阁前的石香炉，当年学子祭拜孔子祖师爷的地方。
Wenchangge, an octagonal wooden structure of two stories. The stone incense burner was where students paid respects to Confucius, father of education.

桂花厅里文脉长
Long literary tradition at Laurel Hall

抱一书屋（南屏私塾）
Baoyi School (Nanping private school)

竹山书院的"所得乃清旷"题额
"A clear mind is what you get", board inscription at Zhushan School

邻溪书屋（关麓私塾）
Lingxi School（Guanlu private school）

第五节　街道与店铺

　　大村必有街，小村亦有店，明清时代的徽州乡村的商业已经繁荣。新安江上的商船给临江的万安古镇带来了格外的繁荣。百年老街，风貌依旧，只是少了往日的喧闹，多了一份真实的回忆。

这样的小木桥，过去的乡村里很常见（婺源县思溪）
Such wooden bridges were once common (Sixi of Wuyuan County)

3.5　Streets and stores

　　Large villages must have streets, and even small villages must have stores. In the Ming and Qing, the business of villages of Huizhou flourished. The merchant ships on the Xinanjiang River brought an unprecedented boom to the old town of Wanan nearby. The century-old street is still what it was, but without its former noisiness and with truer memories.

休宁县万安镇的百年老街，还是当年的模样，只是不见了当年的繁荣。
Century-old street at Wanan of Xiuning County remains what it formerly was, but not its former prosperity.

店门关上了，石板路依旧。
When the store is closed, the slate street is left behind.

旧柜台新商品，生存也不容易
New arrivals at old counter: Life is not easy

万安街紧靠横江，商船带来了当年的繁荣
Wanan Street close to the Hengjiang, where merchant
ships brought back the former prosperity

窄窄的长长的街道
Long and narrow street

这家店面好大，还透着当年的气势
Big store tells a story of old days

"大展鸿图" 的背后……
Behind the "Blueprint"

小狗打破了老街的冷清
Dog breaks the solitude of old street

宏村东边老街
Old street at the east of Hongcun

歙县唐模村的水街，还留存着一段岁月
Water street of Tangmocun of Xixian County preserves the old days

小桥流水人家（卢村）
Stream, bridge, household（Lucun）

第六节　宏村人工古水系

　　六百年前，宏村人先挖水渠引水进村，建立起全村的天然供水网络系统，然后再建房兴村，挖了月沼和南湖，为村庄添了一处水面景色，这种"天人合一"的人居环境的文明理念，正是宏村人工古水系留下的科学、美学、历史的价值。

宏村人工古水系的渠首工程——石碣头
Stone stairs — head of the old water system of Hongcun

3.6　Old water system of Hongcun

　　Six centuries ago, Hongcunans dug a ditch to introduce water to the village, and established a network of natural water supply for the entire village. They then built houses and dug the Crescent Pool and South Lake, adding more water sights to the village. The idea of a living environment that "man lives in harmony with Heaven" was the very scientific, esthetic and historical value left behind by the old water system of Hongcun.

月沼晨曦
Crescent Pool at daybreak

居家日子
Family life

茶行弄口上水圳
Tea goes through the alley to the canal

初冬的南湖不失娇艳
Nanhu Park remains tender and charming in early winter

老屋门前新绿多
New green in front of old house

荷叶田田好凉爽
Cool lotus leaves

南湖的东半湖
East section of South Lake

历史的一角
Corner of history

岁月的印痕
Imprints of past days

秋天的画桥
Pictorial bridge in autumn

寻找远去的家园
Seeking the distant home

纷至沓来
Coming thick and fast

林间的洗衣池（南屏）
Clothes-washing pool in the grove（Nanping）

五百年的生机仍在凝聚（宏村村口古树红杨白果）
Life after five centuries continues（Red poplar and gingko at the entrance to Hongcun）

雄风依旧
Majestic air remains

沧桑的岁月（三元井）
Vicissitudes（Triple well）

　　歙县渔梁坝，重建于明万历年间，坝长143米，底宽27米，顶宽6米，高5米，工程巨大牢固，兼具灌溉、行舟、抗洪之利。
Yuliang dam in She County, rebuilt in Ming dynasty emperor Wanli period, is sized 143m×6m×5m. As an immense and solid water conservancy project, it benefits irrigation, water carriage and flood-preventing.

月朗朗
Moonlight

满山秋色入画来
Pictorial beauty in autumn

古村惊艳
Exceptional beauty of old village

图书在版编目（CIP）数据

徽州老房子／汪森强著 . —南京：江苏凤凰美术出
版社，2008.5（2019.8 重印）
ISBN 978-7-5344-2236-2

Ⅰ. 徽… Ⅱ. 汪… Ⅲ. 古建筑—建筑艺术—徽
州地区 Ⅳ.TU-092.2

中国版本图书馆 CIP 数据核字（2008）第 062036 号

策　　划　汪森强
摄　　影　卢庭芳
制　　图　李　华　万建安
英文翻译　李长生　黄小林　李爱珍
责任编辑　毛晓剑　龚　婷
装帧设计　毛晓剑
责任校对　刁海裕
责任监印　生　嫄

书　　名　徽州老房子
著　　者　汪森强
出版发行　江苏凤凰美术出版社（南京市中央路 165 号　邮编：210009）
出版社网址　http://www.jsmscbs.com.cn
制　　版　南京新华丰制版有限公司
印　　刷　南京凯德印刷有限公司
开　　本　889mm × 1194mm　1/32
印　　张　6.5
版　　次　2008 年 5 月第 1 版　2019 年 8 月第 11 次印刷
标准书号　ISBN 978-7-5344-2236-2
定　　价　65.00 元

营销部电话　025-68155790　营销部地址　南京市中央路 165 号
江苏凤凰美术出版社图书凡印装错误可向承印厂调换

《唐肃宗宴官图》（前厅额枋）　Emperor Suzong of the Tang Entertains Officials at Banquet（on the

以四桌琴棋书画的聚乐场面，渲染一种君臣同乐、轻松开心的气氛，配上剃头烧水的生活

The whole woodcut displays a scene in which the emperor and his ministers have a pleasant time usi
and is natural and full of real-life zest.

《百子闹元宵》（前厅仪门之上画板）　A Hundred Children Celebrate the Lantern Festival（on the

整幅画面分作五组演艺活动场景，自左至右，坐旱船、舞龙、演戏、舞狮、鲤鱼跳龙门。
富立体感，雕工细腻，洋溢着万民同乐、喜迎新春的快乐祥和的节日气氛，是一幅少有的艺术

The drawing has five scenes of artistic shows: from left to right, land boating, dragon dance, opera, li
drums and gongs, light firecrackers, carry lanterns, and swing flags, and hail. The players are of different
an all-happy atmosphere of the Spring Festival season, and thus is an artistic rarity.

《郭子仪上寿》（后厅额枋）　Guo Ziyi's Birthday（on the column of the back hall）

郭子仪（公元697－781），唐代大将，屡建奇功，又屡削兵权。郭公心胸开阔，用之则行
人。"郭子仪上寿"成了民间崇拜郭子仪德行、劝戒世人宽容处世的艺术题材。承志堂后厅额木

Guo Ziyi (697－781), general of the Tang, who achieved many military deeds and who was depriv
seeking recluse when he is out of power. He had "seven sons and eight son-in-laws", and was highly r
and happiness. "Guo Ziyi's Birthday" is a popular theme of art that propagates virtue and tolerance. In
deliver a message of fortune and longevity.

《百忍图》　A Hundred Ren Characters

唐代寿人张公艺九世同居，家族和睦。唐高宗询其治家之道，张公艺书写了100多个"忍"
字呈复，唐高宗认为很有道理，赏其缣帛。

Zhang Gongyi of the Tang had a happy family living together for nine generations. When Emperor
Gaozong asked him how such a large family was maintained, Zhang wrote more than a hundred ren
(tolerance) characters in reply. The emperor sang high praise, and awarded Zhang with silk and fabrics.

column of the front hall)

场景，整个画面更显得自然逼真，雅趣盎然。

g four tables of flute, chess, calligraphy and drawing, accompanied by barber shop and boiling water scenes,

board of the door to the front hall)

吹唢呐、敲锣鼓、放鞭炮、举花灯、摇旗呐喊者跃然画面、神态各异、栩栩如生、疏密有间，极

精品。

n dance and the Carp-Leap-into-the-Dragon-Gate game. One can see those who blow the surnay, beat

ostures of liveliness. The design of the drawing emphasizes spacing and fine carving. The drawing radiates

舍之则藏，无怨无悔，适时行乐，七子八婿，显贵于朝，寿至八十五，历代推之为有德有福之

木雕《郭子仪上寿》，"寿"字柱础，厅堂上"福禄寿"三星陈设，暗合祈祝长辈长寿的美意。

d of his military power for several times. He had an open mind, exerting every effort while in power and

spected at the official court. He lived until he was eighty-five years old, a symbol of a man of great virtue

he drawing, the shou (longevity) character plinth, and the furnishings with the fu, lu and shou characters,